HOW TO
DECORATE your HOME
WITH PLASTIC CANVAS

What better way to add distinctive decorative touches to your house than with plastic canvas! Without a doubt, there's not another craft as versatile and unique. In How to Decorate Your Home with Plastic Canvas, *you'll find an abundance of projects to adorn your walls, bedrooms, bathrooms, tables, doors, and every nook and cranny! More than 65 projects await your creative talents, along with helpful decorating tips. You'll love the charming accents — welcoming wreaths, beautiful baskets, pretty picture frames, and much more. So what are you waiting for? Gather your supplies and indulge yourself with these sensational stitching projects!*

LEISURE ARTS, INC.
and
OXMOOR HOUSE, INC.

HOW TO
DECORATE
your HOME
WITH PLASTIC CANVAS

EDITORIAL STAFF

Vice President and Editor-in-Chief:
Anne Van Wagner Childs
Executive Director: Sandra Graham Case
Editorial Director: Susan Frantz Wiles
Publications Director: Susan White Sullivan
Creative Art Director: Gloria Bearden
Design Director: Patricia Wallenfang Sowers

PRODUCTION
Special Projects Editor: Donna Brown Hill
Senior Production Assistant: JoAnn Dickson Forrest
Production Assistants: Karla Edgar, Teal Lee Elliott,
Merrilee Gasaway, and Janie Wright

EDITORIAL
Managing Editor: Linda L. Trimble
Associate Editors: Shelby D. Brewer and
Stacey Robertson Marshall
Copy Editor: Terri Leming Davidson

ART
Crafts Art Director: Rhonda Hodge Shelby
Senior Production Artist: Chris Meux
Production Artists: Rebecca J. Hester, Mindy Reynolds,
John Rose, Wendy Willets, and Karen Wilson
Photography Stylists: Ellen J. Clifton, Sondra Daniel,
Karen Hall, Tiffany Huffman, Elizabeth Lackey, and
Janna Laughlin
Publishing Systems Administrator: Cindy Lumpkin
Publishing Systems Assistant: Myra Means

PROMOTIONS
Managing Editor: Alan Caudle
Associate Editor: Steve M. Cooper
Designer: Dale Rowett
Art Director: Linda Lovette Smart

BUSINESS STAFF

Publisher: Rick Barton
Vice President and General Manager: Thomas L. Carlisle
Vice President, Finance: Tom Siebenmorgen
Director of Corporate Planning and Development:
Laticia Mull Cornett
Vice President, Retail Marketing: Bob Humphrey
Vice President, National Accounts: Pam Stebbins

Retail Marketing Director: Margaret Sweetin
General Merchandise Manager: Cathy Laird
Vice President, Operations: Jim Dittrich
Distribution Director: Rob Thieme
Retail Customer Service Manager: Wanda Price
Print Production Manager: Fred F. Pruss

Hardcover ISBN 1-57486-164-6
Softcover ISBN 1-57486-165-4

10 9 8 7 6 5 4 3 2 1

TABLE OF CONTENTS

first impressions

Say your warmest "welcome" with a handmade greeting at your front door or the entry hall. It's easy to create any of our featured wreaths — just add ribbons, faux flowers, and plastic canvas stitchery to plain store-bought wreaths. Easy-to-stitch butterflies are perky additions to a gathering of florals. For a "tweet" greeting, nestle a framed sampling of birdhouses amid a bunch of springtime flowers, or personalize your wreath with family photos displayed in lovely frames. A "neighborhood" of tiny dimensional houses will charm friends, and a quartet of colorful angels is accented with flowing ribbon for a heavenly "hello!"

Instructions on pages 32-37

DESIGNER TIP

*"Plastic canvas magnets make great embellishments for wreaths —
and there are hundreds of designs available. Look through your Leisure Arts
magazines and leaflets for inspiration. We usually show magnets in themed
sets, which are perfect for accenting wreaths. You can even mix and match
sets to suit your decorating style or to personalize a wreath for a friend."*

Your home—
a reflection of you

Your home is a reflection of you — the person you are and the things you love. Whether your decorating style is traditional, modern, elegant, casual, or an eclectic combination, your home should be a place of comfort and refuge.

Little things mean a lot, and handmade touches really make your house a home. For the living room, a small mirror is framed with a lovely pastel design created using only two stitches. Display a photograph of your beloved homeplace in an easy standing picture frame. Perfect for welcoming guests, this Victorian-style cottage doorstop features a dimensional picket fence and lush "landscaping."

Instructions on pages 38-40

den

An eye-catching accent for the den (or any room), this warm sunflower clock is "planted" in a clay pot. With our handy chairside catchall, you'll never have to search for the TV remote again! The caddy even comes with its own built-in coaster. A sunny storage box for stationery, household receipts, or odds-and-ends is at home wherever you place it.

DESIGNER TIP
"Classic color combinations can be repeated in many types of projects to create a coordinated look within a room. Mixing blues and yellows is a great way to bring sunshine to any room. Why not stitch some of the other projects in this book (such as frames, bookends, etc.) using these appealing hues?"

Instructions on pages 41-45

kitchen

Bring a fresh, new look to your kitchen
with accessories inspired by spring's prettiest
flower ... the tulip. Our doily is easily made by stitching
together plastic canvas hexagons. Slip a floral insert
into a snap-together plastic mug to enjoy that first cup
of morning coffee. The cheerful magnets stitch up
in no time! As useful as it is decorative, the
flower-embellished napkin holder brightens
a breakfast nook.

Instructions on pages 46-47

bedroom and bath

You'll find lots of pretty posies in this charming bed and bath collection!
Step onto our elegant rug, which is made by combining five-mesh blocks stitched
with two strands of yarn. Give the bathroom a little flair with a tissue box cover,
a potpourri container, an embellished basket, and lifelike daffodils arranged
in a simple vase. Each stitched piece coordinates with the bedroom
rug, so your decor flows from one room to the other!

Instructions on pages 48-51

DESIGNER TIP
"Try stitching the floral rug squares separately. You can then
frame each one individually and arrange them on the wall, or
finish the edges with overcast stitches and hang them on a wide
ribbon, one above the other. What a pretty designer touch!"

Pretty, yet practical

One of the best things about plastic canvas needlework is that it's pretty as well as practical. Guests in your home will discover your handiwork atop tissue boxes, beneath drinking glasses, and on the shelf propping up your favorite books. With so many options from which to choose, you'll love decorating every room with accents you can really use!

Coasters offer more than just protection for your furniture — they can enhance the decorative theme of your home, too! For a house with country decor, heart-trimmed coasters in a matching basket make a great addition. If your style is more casual, tropical fish with bold contrasts are most appealing. Patterned coasters in deep tones complement traditional homes, and eye-catching animal prints edged in fringe add fun to a contemporary theme.

Instructions on pages 52-54

15

bookends

Where books abound, these nifty holders can be found! Warm up a corner
of the family room with homespun bookends featuring pretty flowers and a timeless
phrase. Prop up those cookbooks using these cheery strawberry basket bookends,
or add traditional style with a geometric design to cover metal bookends.

Instructions on pages 55-57

tissue box covers

No matter what your style, we've got the tissue box cover for you! Geometric patterns are at home in a bedroom or bathroom, or keep it simple with a single color of yarn stitched into a textured finish. Animal prints are a favorite trend, and our leopard-spot and tiger-stripe cover is especially fun. For a den or boy's room, choose an equestrian design. A lighthearted addition to any room, birdhouses make a cover extra "tweet."

Instructions on pages 58-62

hold everything!

Versatile yet unique, plastic canvas crafts are more than just pretty decorations — they can be handy containers as well! For example, stitch a box in soft country colors to store your sewing notions. Display candy in a small multi-colored basket, or hide those precious pearls in a pretty heart-shaped box. Last but not least, let plants show their true beauty in a basket-shaped planter.

DESIGNER TIP
"Stitch your initials on any of these plastic canvas containers to add a personal touch, or stitch the initials of that special someone and give as a gift. Also, you can make a container more meaningful by backstitching a favorite verse or quote on the bottom or back."

Instructions on pages 63-67

Unexpected touches

It's the little things that count, especially when it comes to decorating your home. Plastic canvas is a great way to customize every room. These projects, however, will do more than just add a personal touch — they'll convey personality, and lots of it! With plastic canvas, you can create anything, from a lovely ladybug plant poke to a plastic canvas potpourri bottle.

An adorable little ladybug will liven up any plant! Surrounded by a bright red border, a heart-shaped plaque captures the comfortable feeling of home. With the money you saved making these inexpensive creations, why not toss your spare change into our multi-colored coin box? Or make a room smell sweet with a plastic canvas bottle filled with potpourri. A unique tiger-lily candlestick holder will add character and charm to any room.

Instructions on pages 68-71

23

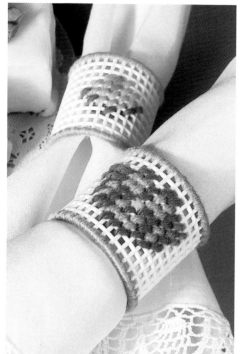

DESIGNER TIP
"All the items in this section would make great last-minute gifts for your friends — they'd love
using them to decorate their homes. That is, of course, if you can part with them yourself!"

Dainty potpourri cubes stitched on white canvas are "scent-sational," and napkin rings displaying pretty pink and purple flowers make ordinary napkins look exquisite! Good things come in small packages, as shown by the little canvas house. It's not only cute but also useful — you can take the roof off to store sweetener packets. Also handy is the blue and white notepad holder. Last but not least, delicate 10-mesh trims dress up fabric-covered baskets.

Instructions on pages 72-74

25

deck the walls

"Deck the walls with boughs of holly, fa la la la .... " Wait a minute ... who needs holly when you've got plastic canvas! These lovely wall pieces make your home festive no matter what the season. Accented with warm shades of green and burgundy on 10-mesh canvas, this framed picture is simply "pear-fect!" Display a cherished photograph in a charming picture frame with variegated yarn stitched over cording for dimension. The gold and ecru color-coordinated clock and sampler will no doubt attract compliments — both demonstrate exceptional pattern stitches.

DESIGNER TIP
"Any of the stitches in the sampler would look great on a clock or picture frame! Experiment with color schemes to evoke different moods. For example, try combining blue with white or yellow for a bright and cheery look. Or perhaps try stitching soothing greens to create a calming effect, reds for energy, etc."

Instructions on pages 75-78

27

baby talk

The nursery will always be the most precious room in the house! Pastel blocks march across the bottom of a photo frame just for baby, and a door hanger whispers a request for quiet. Get things organized with a charming box to hold diapers or a tissue box cover bearing heart designs. Dimensional baby blocks, rocking horses, and a bank add special touches.

Instructions on pages 79-84

†ot to teen

It can be a real jungle in there, but kids love having a place to call their own! Our wild and crazy collection will delight tots and teens alike with fun animal motifs and bright colors. A cute monkey door hanger proclaims that this is "My Room." Decorate a dresser or shelf with a whimsical frog sitter whose floppy legs are made by tying strands of yarn together. Our tropical monkey frame, nicely detailed on 10 mesh canvas, is perfect for portraying a picture of a fun time with friends.

first impressions

BUTTERFLY WREATH
(Shown on page 4)

Butterfly Size: Approx. 3$\frac{1}{2}$"w x 2$\frac{3}{4}$"h each

Supplies: Worsted weight yarn, 10$\frac{1}{2}$" x 13$\frac{1}{2}$" sheets of clear 7 mesh plastic canvas, #16 tapestry needle, 13" dia. grapevine wreath, 24" length of 1$\frac{1}{2}$"w wire-edge ribbon, silk flowers, artificial ivy, black cloth-covered wire, wooden skewers (optional), and craft glue

Stitches Used: Backstitch, Overcast Stitch, and Tent Stitch

Instructions: Follow charts to cut and stitch desired number of Butterfly pieces. For each Butterfly, cut two 3" lengths of wire for antennas. Glue antennas to back of Butterfly and shape as shown in photo.

Tie ribbon into a bow and trim ends. Glue bow to Wreath. If desired, glue Butterflies to wooden skewers. Glue ivy, flowers, and Butterflies to Wreath.

Designs by Dick Martin.

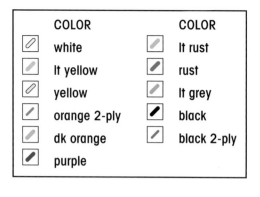

COLOR		COLOR	
⊘	white	⊘	lt rust
⊘	lt yellow	⊘	rust
⊘	yellow	⊘	lt grey
⊘	orange 2-ply	⊘	black
⊘	dk orange	⊘	black 2-ply
⊘	purple		

Butterfly #1 (25 x 25 threads)

Butterfly #2 (34 x 34 threads)

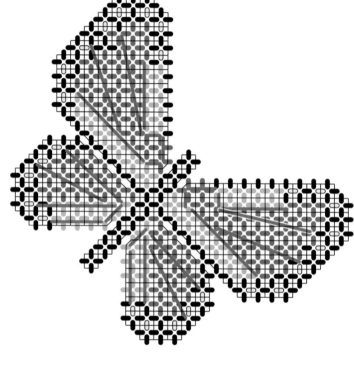

Butterfly #3 (14 x 14 threads)

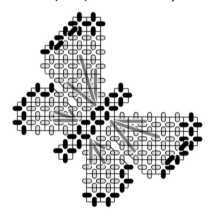

HOME TWEET HOME WREATH

(Shown on page 5)

Sampler Size: Approx. 5"w x 7"h

Supplies: Embroidery floss, one 8¼" x 11" sheet of white 14 mesh perforated plastic, #24 tapestry needle, 16" dia. grapevine wreath, two yds of 2½"w sheer wire-edge ribbon, silk flowers, artificial greenery, frame with 5" x 7" opening, paint (optional), and craft glue

Stitch Used: Cross Stitch

Instructions: Center and stitch design on perforated plastic using three strands of embroidery floss. If desired, paint frame. Trim excess canvas and glue stitched piece inside frame.

Tie ribbon into a bow and trim ends. Glue bow to Wreath. Glue greenery, flowers, and framed piece to Wreath.

Design by Deborah Lambein.

Home Tweet Home

COLOR	DMC#
yellow	744
pink	899
lavender	210
lt blue	3761
blue	799
lt green	472
green	913
brown	840

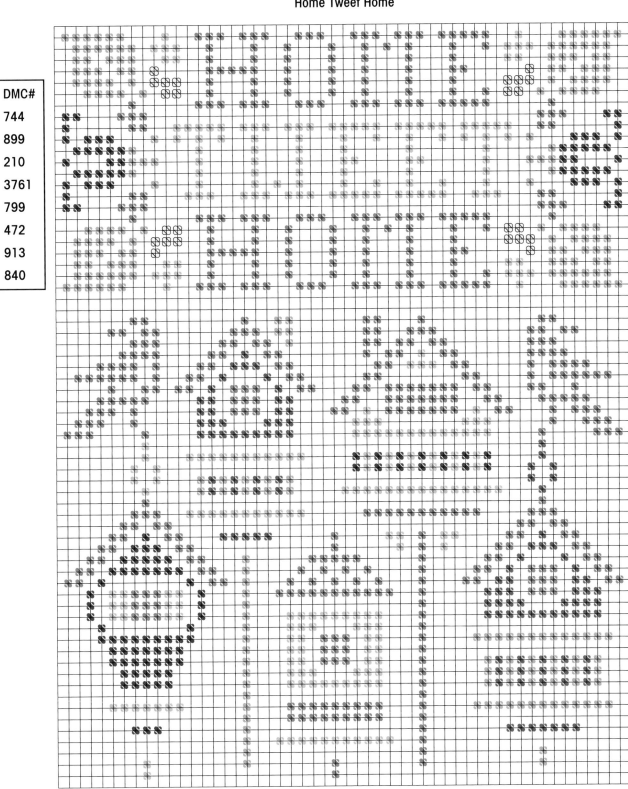

FAMILY PHOTO WREATH

(Shown on page 5)

Frame Size: Approx. 2³/₄"w x 3"h each

Supplies: Worsted weight yarn, green DMC Embroidery Floss #562, one 10¹/₂" x 13¹/₂" sheet of clear 7 mesh plastic canvas, #16 tapestry needle, 13"w x 11"h heart-shaped grapevine wreath, two yds of 2"w wire-edge ribbon, silk flowers, artificial greenery, photographs, and craft glue

Stitches Used: Backstitch, French Knot, Overcast Stitch, and Tent Stitch

Instructions: Follow charts to cut and stitch Frame pieces. Before adding Backstitches and French Knots, cover unworked edges of Frames using matching color yarn.

Tie ribbon into a bow and trim ends. Glue bow to wreath. Trim photographs and glue to back of Frames. Glue greenery, flowers, and Frames to Wreath.

Designs by Nancy Dorman.

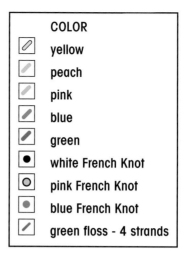

	COLOR
▨	yellow
▨	peach
▨	pink
▨	blue
▨	green
●	white French Knot
◉	pink French Knot
●	blue French Knot
▨	green floss - 4 strands

Frame #1 (22 x 17 threads)

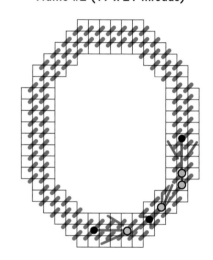

Frame #2 (17 x 21 threads)

Frame #3 (19 x 19 threads)

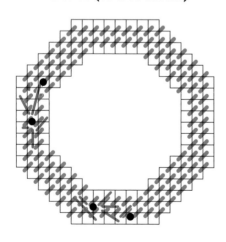

Frame #4 (20 x 20 threads)

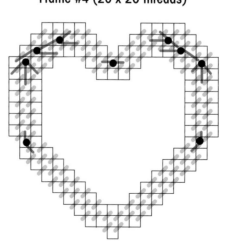

Frame #5 (17 x 22 threads)

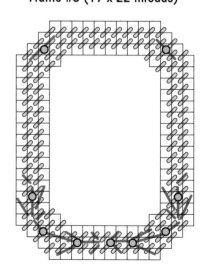

ANGEL WREATH

(Shown on page 5)

Angel Size: 3¼"w x 3¾"h

Supplies: Worsted weight yarn, 10½" x 13½" sheets of clear 7 mesh plastic canvas, #16 tapestry needle, 12" dia. white twig wreath, two 24" lengths of 1½"w wire-edge ribbon, additional ribbons in two yd lengths of various widths and colors, silver chenille stems, and craft glue

Stitches Used: Backstitch, Cross Stitch, French Knot, Loose Overcast Stitch, Overcast Stitch, and Tent Stitch

Instructions: Follow charts to cut and stitch pieces to make desired number of Angels. Match symbols to join pieces together as follows.

Using white yarn, join Left Wing and Right Wing to Back between ×'s and ★'s through three thicknesses of plastic canvas. Cut a 8" length of silver chenille stem. Thread one end of stem under stitches on wrong side of Back at ▲. Refer to photo and bend chenille stem to form halo.

Referring to photo for yarn color, join Front to Back with wrong sides together. For hair, use desired color yarn to work Loose Overcast Stitches between ■'s.

Tie wire-edge ribbons into bows and trim ends. Glue bows to Wreath. Glue remaining ribbons to Wreath. Glue Angels to Wreath.

LOOSE OVERCAST STITCH

Worked on top of completed Overcast Stitches, this stitch is worked like the Overcast Stitch to form loops approximately ⅛" high. It may be necessary to go through the same hole more than once to get an even coverage, especially at the corners.

	COLOR
	white
	peach
	pink
	desired color
	desired color
●	blue 2-ply French Knot

Left Wing (9 x 12 threads)

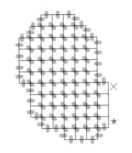

Right Wing (9 x 12 threads)

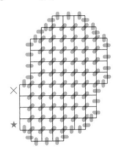

Front (21 x 21 threads)

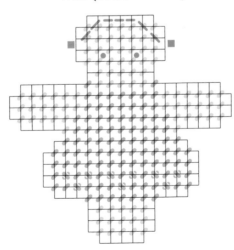

Back (21 x 21 threads)

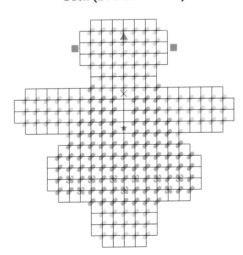

HOUSE WREATH

(Shown on page 5)

House Size: Approx. 3¼"w x 3¼"h each
Welcome Sign Size: 5¾"w x 1½"h
Supplies: Worsted weight yarn, one 10½" x 13½" sheet of clear 7 mesh plastic canvas, #16 tapestry needle, 15" dia. grapevine wreath, two yds of 2½"w wire-edge ribbon, artificial ivy, and craft glue
Stitches Used: Backstitch, Cross Stitch, French Knot, Gobelin Stitch, Overcast Stitch, and Tent Stitch
Instructions: Follow charts to cut and stitch pieces. Using dk blue yarn, cover unworked edges of Welcome Sign.

For Gold House, match ★'s to place Roof on top of House. Using brown yarn, join unworked edges of Roof to House. Match ✚'s to place Fence on top of House. Using green yarn, join bottom edge of Fence to House.

For Yellow House, match ◆'s to place Front on top of Back. Glue Front to Back.

For Peach House, match ✳'s to place Front on top of Back. Glue Front to Back.

For Blue House, match ▲'s to place Porch on top of House. Using tan yarn, join top edge of Porch to House. Using green yarn, tack bottom edge of Porch to House.

Tie ribbon into a bow and trim ends. Glue bow to Wreath. Glue ivy and Houses to Wreath.

Designs by Kooler Design Studio.

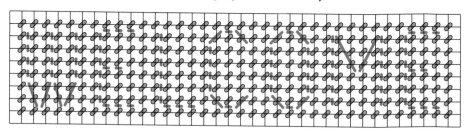

	COLOR		COLOR
✏	white	✏	rust
✏	ecru	✏	tan
✏	yellow	✏	brown
✏	peach	✏	grey
✏	gold	✏	dk grey
✏	blue	○	yellow French Knot
✏	dk blue	◉	orange French Knot
✏	green	●	red French Knot
✏	dk green	●	purple French Knot

Welcome Sign (38 x 10 threads)

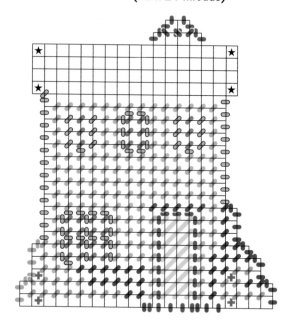

Gold House (22 x 24 threads)

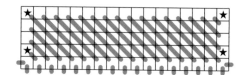

Gold House Roof (18 x 6 threads)

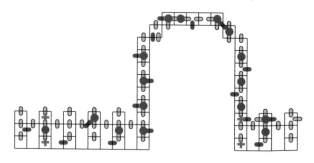

Gold House Fence (24 x 12 threads)

Yellow House Back (22 x 19 threads)

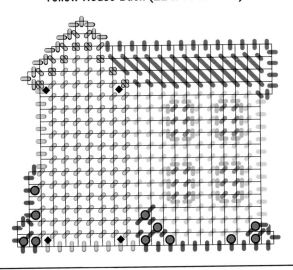

Yellow House Front (10 x 19 threads)

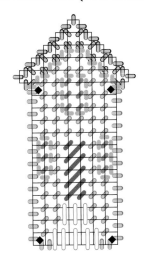

Peach House Front (14 x 23 threads)

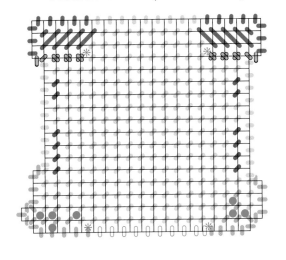

Peach House Back (21 x 18 threads)

Blue House Porch (25 x 14 threads)

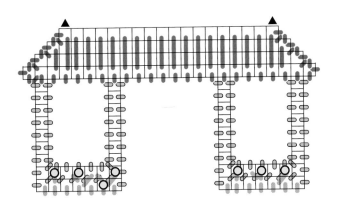

Blue House (19 x 21 threads)

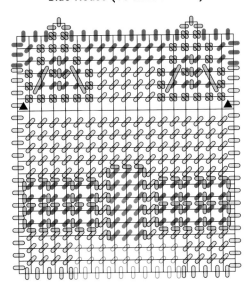

37

Your home — a reflection of you

COTTAGE DOORSTOP
(Shown on page 7)

Size: 11¼"w x 8"h x 4"d

Supplies: Worsted weight yarn, three 10½" x 13½" sheets of clear 7 mesh plastic canvas, #16 tapestry needle, 7½"w x 3½"h x 2⅛"d brick, plastic wrap, and craft glue

Stitches Used: Backstitch, French Knot, Gobelin Stitch, Overcast Stitch, and Tent Stitch

Instructions: Follow charts to cut and stitch pieces. Cut a 56 x 27 thread piece of plastic canvas for Front. Cut a 56 x 17 thread piece of plastic canvas for Bottom. Front and Bottom are not stitched.

Using green yarn, join Front to Top along long edges. Join Back to Top. Join Bottom to Front and Back. Join one Side to Front, Back, Top, and Bottom.

Wrap brick with plastic wrap and insert brick into Doorstop. Join remaining Side to Doorstop.

Using matching color yarn, match ■'s and ★'s to tack Short Fence to Cottage. Matching ▲'s and ✳'s, tack Long Fence to Cottage.

Glue Cottage to Doorstop Front.

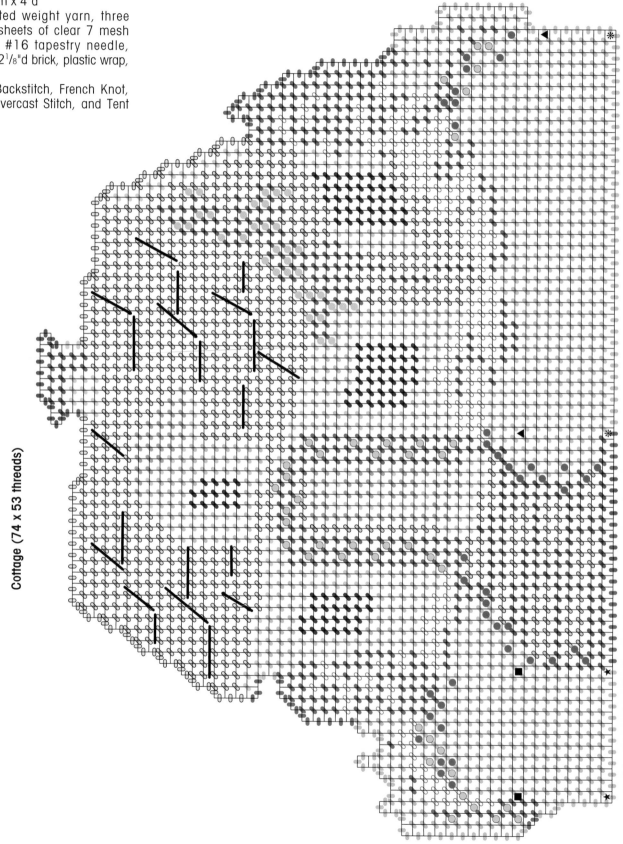

Cottage (74 x 53 threads)

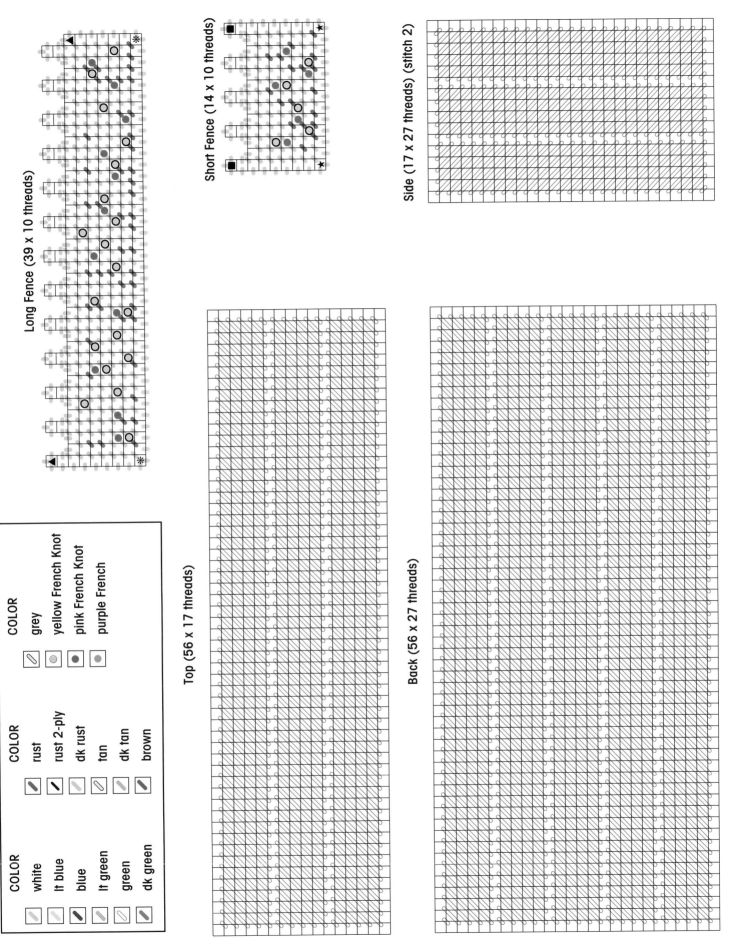

Long Fence (39 x 10 threads)

Short Fence (14 x 10 threads)

Side (17 x 27 threads) (stitch 2)

Top (56 x 17 threads)

Back (56 x 27 threads)

COLOR		COLOR		COLOR	
white		rust		grey	
lt blue		rust 2-ply		yellow French Knot	
blue		dk rust		pink French Knot	
lt green		tan		purple French	
green		dk tan			
dk green		brown			

SQUARE FRAME

(Shown on page 6)

Size: 4$\frac{1}{2}$"w x 4$\frac{1}{2}$"h

(Mirror opening is 2"w x 2$\frac{1}{4}$"h.)

Supplies: Worsted weight yarn, one 10$\frac{1}{2}$" x 13$\frac{1}{2}$" sheet of clear 7 mesh stiff plastic canvas, #16 tapestry needle, mirror to fit opening, sawtooth hanger, and craft glue

Stitches Used: Overcast Stitch and Tent Stitch

Instructions: Follow chart to cut and stitch Square Frame. Glue mirror and sawtooth hanger to back of Frame.

RECTANGLE FRAME

(Shown on page 6)

Size: 5$\frac{3}{4}$"w x 5$\frac{1}{4}$"h

(Photo opening is 3$\frac{3}{4}$"w x 3$\frac{1}{4}$"h.)

Supplies: Worsted weight yarn, one 10$\frac{1}{2}$" x 13$\frac{1}{2}$" sheet of clear 7 mesh stiff plastic canvas, and #16 tapestry needle

Stitches Used: Gobelin Stitch, Overcast Stitch, and Tent Stitch

Instructions: Follow chart to cut and stitch Rectangle Frame. Cut a piece of plastic canvas 39 x 35 threads for Back. Cut a piece of plastic canvas 12 x 35 threads for Stand Top. Cut a piece of plastic canvas 12 x 21 threads for Stand Bottom. Back, Stand Top, and Stand Bottom are not stitched.

Refer to Diagram to construct Frame. Using blue yarn, join Stand Top to Stand Bottom along one short edge. Join Front to Back along unworked edges of Front. Tack Stand to Back. Cover unworked edge of Back.

Designs by Mary Billeaudeau.

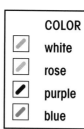

COLOR	
	white
	rose
	purple
	blue

Square Frame (31 x 31 threads)

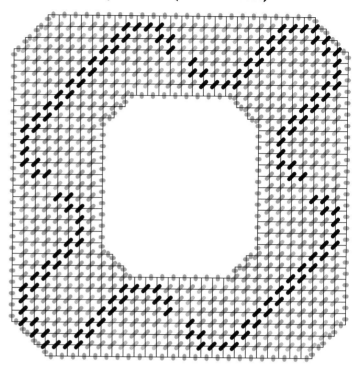

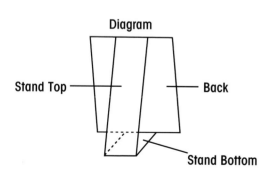

Diagram

Stand Top — Back

Stand Bottom

Rectangle Frame (39 x 35 threads)

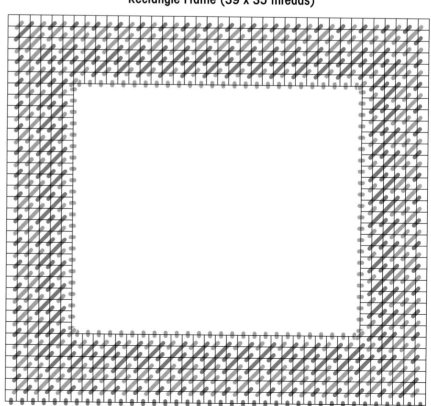

40

UNFLOWER CLOCK

(Shown on page 8)

Size: 8¹/₂"w x 15¹/₂"h x 4"d

Supplies: Worsted weight yarn, one 10¹/₂" x 13¹/₂" sheet of clear 7 mesh plastic canvas, 4¹/₄" dia. Darice® plastic canvas circle, #16 tapestry needle, plaster of paris, battery operated clock movement for ¹/₄" thick clock face, three 4" lengths of 20 gauge floral wire, 3¹/₂" dia. clay flowerpot with saucer, 10" length of ¹/₄" dia. wooden dowel, 12 gold beads, paint (optional), Spanish moss (optional), and craft glue

Stitches Used: Backstitch, Gobelin Stitch, Overcast Stitch, Scotch Stitch, and Tent Stitch

Instructions: Cut and remove middle of Flower Center from plastic canvas circle along pink cutting line. Follow charts to cut and stitch pieces. Using brown yarn, cover unworked edges of Flower Center.

If desired, paint dowel. Glue flowerpot to saucer. Follow manufacturer's instructions to mix plaster of paris and pour into flowerpot. Insert dowel into plaster.

Using white yarn, join short edges of Band together to form a cylinder. Glue Band to Flowerpot. If desired, paint plaster and cover with Spanish moss.

Glue Flower Petals to back of Flower Center. Glue beads to Flower Center. Insert clock movement into Flower Center. Follow manufacturer's instructions to assemble clock. Glue dowel to back of Flower.

Glue one floral wire piece to back of each Leaf. After glue has dried, bend Leaves as shown in photo. Glue Leaves to dowel.

Design by Conn Baker Gibney.

Band

(7 x 80 threads)

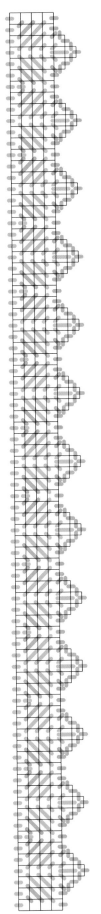

Flower Petal

(8 x 18 threads)

(stitch 16)

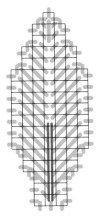

	COLOR		COLOR
	white		green
	gold		brown
	orange		dk brown
	lt green		black
	lt green 2-ply		

Leaf

(16 x 31 threads)

(stitch 3)

Flower Center

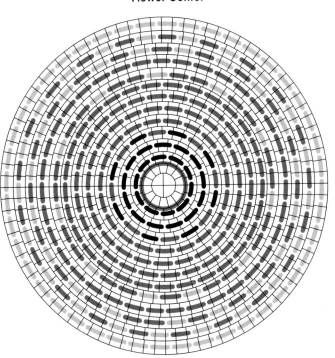

TV CATCHALL

(Shown on page 9)

Size: 7"w x 4¹/₂"h x 9¹/₄"d

Supplies: Worsted weight yarn, two 10¹/₂" x 13¹/₂" sheets of clear 7 mesh plastic canvas, #16 tapestry needle, cork or felt (optional), and craft glue (optional)

Stitches Used: Cross Stitch, Gobelin Stitch, Overcast Stitch, and Tent Stitch

Instructions: Follow charts to cut and stitch pieces, leaving stitches in shaded areas unworked. Using blue yarn, match symbols to join pieces together as follows.

Join short edges of Front to Sides. Join Back to Sides. Join Back and Sides to Bottom. Work stitches in yellow shaded area to join Front to Bottom. Join remaining unworked edges of Front to Bottom.

Work stitches in green shaded areas to join Section Dividers to front of Divider #3. Matching ■'s and ✳'s, join Divider #3 to Sides. Work stitches in pink shaded areas to join Divider #3 and Section Dividers to Bottom.

Work stitches in purple shaded area to join Section Dividers to Back of Divider #2. Matching ♥'s and ♦'s, join Divider #2 to Sides. Join Divider #2 to Bottom.

Matching ★'s and ▲'s, work remaining shaded stitches to join Divider #1 to Sides and Bottom.

If backing is desired for coaster, cut cork or felt slightly smaller than coaster and glue to back of coaster.

Design by Tina Chaney.

Bottom (46 x 62 threads)

Front
(6 x 46 threads)

Divider #1
(6 x 46 threads)

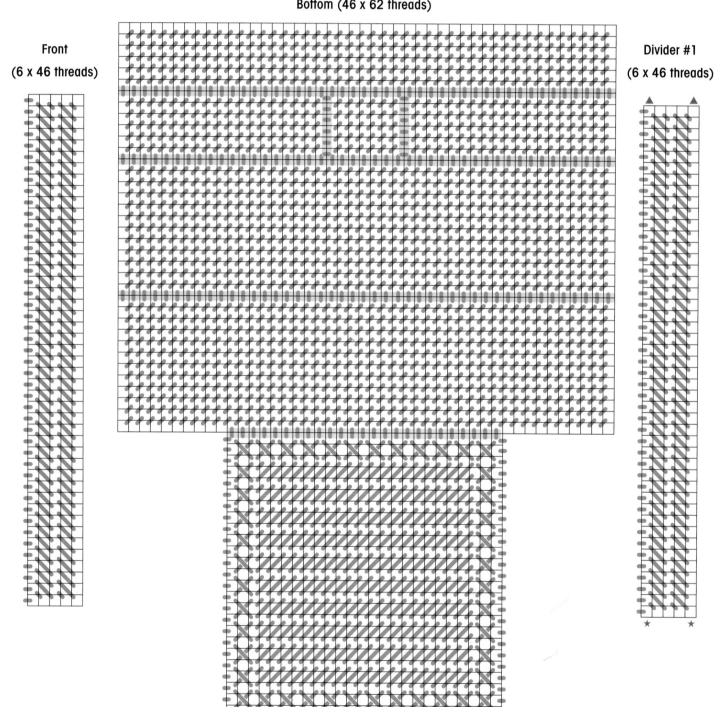

COLOR

blue

Side #1
(37 x 30 threads)

Divider #2 (46 x 16 threads)

Side #2
(37 x 30 threads)

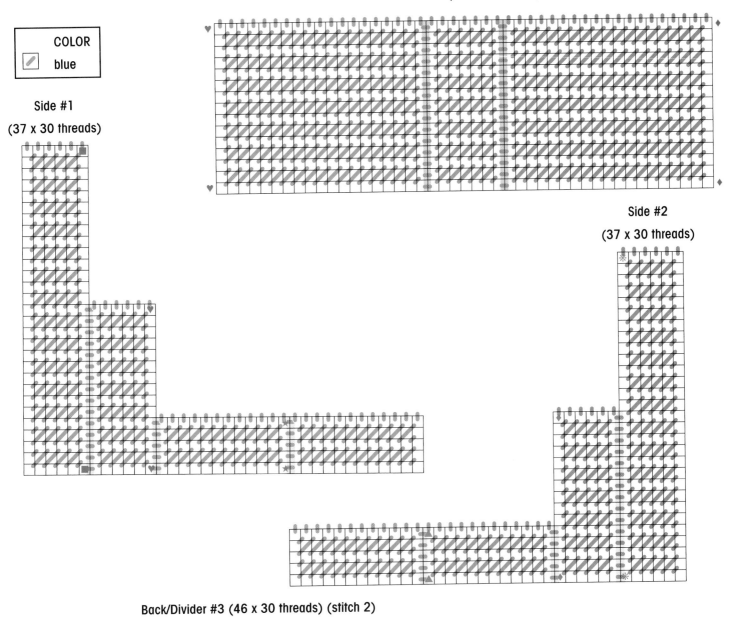

Back/Divider #3 (46 x 30 threads) (stitch 2)

Section Divider
(6 x 16 threads)
(stitch 2)

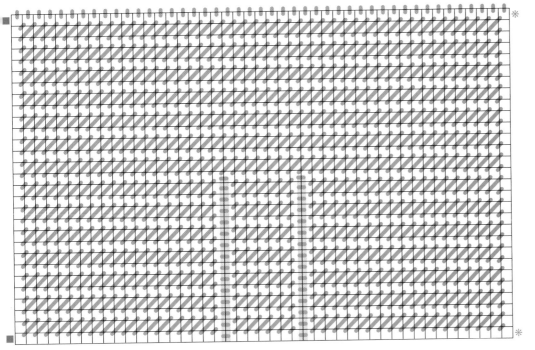

GRANNY SQUARE BOX

(Shown on page 9)

Size: 9¾"w x 6"h x 4¼"d

Supplies: Worsted weight yarn, three 10½" x 13½" sheets of clear 7 mesh stiff plastic canvas, and #16 tapestry needle

Stitches Used: Backstitch, Gobelin Stitch, Modified Eyelet Stitch, Overcast Stitch, and Tent Stitch

Instructions: Follow charts to cut and stitch pieces. Cut a 62 x 26 thread piece of plastic canvas for Bottom. Bottom is not stitched.

Using blue yarn, join Front to Sides. Join Back to Sides. Join Bottom to Front, Back, and Sides.

Join Top Side pieces together along short edges, alternating Side #1 and Side #2 pieces to form a rectangle. Join Top to Top Sides.

Design by Georgia A. Appenzellar.

	COLOR
✎	yellow
✎	orange
✎	blue
✎	tan
✎	brown

Side

(26 x 38 threads) (stitch 2)

Front/Back

(62 x 38 threads) (stitch 2)

Top Side #1

(28 x 14 threads) (stitch 2)

Top Side #2

(64 x 14 threads) (stitch 2)

Top

(64 x 28 threads)

TULIP DOILY

(Shown on page 10)

Size: 14"w x 14"h

Supplies: Worsted weight yarn, seven 5" Uniek® hexagon plastic canvas shapes, and #16 tapestry needle

Stitches Used: Gobelin Stitch, Overcast Stitch, and Tent Stitch

Instructions: Follow chart to stitch pieces. Using green yarn, join Doily Sections together. Cover unworked edges of Doily.

Design by Michele Wilcox.

TULIP MAGNET

(Shown on page 11)

Size: 2½"w x 3½"h

Supplies: Worsted weight yarn, or 10½" x 13½" sheet of clear 7 mes plastic canvas, #16 tapestry needl magnetic strip, and craft glue

Stitches Used: Gobelin Stitch, Overca Stitch, and Tent Stitch

Instructions: Follow chart to cut and stitc Magnet. Glue magnetic strip to back stitched piece.

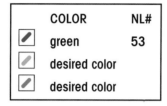

	COLOR	NL#
▨	green	53
▨	desired color	
▨	desired color	

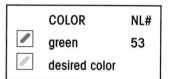

	COLOR	NL#
▨	green	53
▨	desired color	

Doily Section

(stitch 7)

Magnet

(18 x 23 threads)

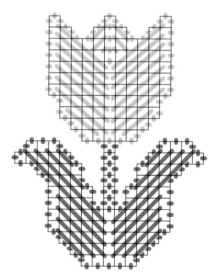

46

JL!P MUG INSERT

(Shown on page 11)

Size: 3½"h x 3" dia.

Supplies: Worsted weight yarn, one 10½" x 13½" sheet of clear 7 mesh plastic canvas, #16 tapestry needle, and green Crafter's Pride® Mugs-Your-Way™

Stitches Used: Cross Stitch, Gobelin Stitch, Overcast Stitch, and Tent Stitch

Instructions: Follow chart to cut and stitch Mug Insert. Using ecru yarn, join ends together to form a cylinder.

Design by Judy Hill.

	COLOR	NL#
/	ecru	39
/	yellow	19
/	rose	05
/	green	53

Mug Insert (64 x 24 threads)

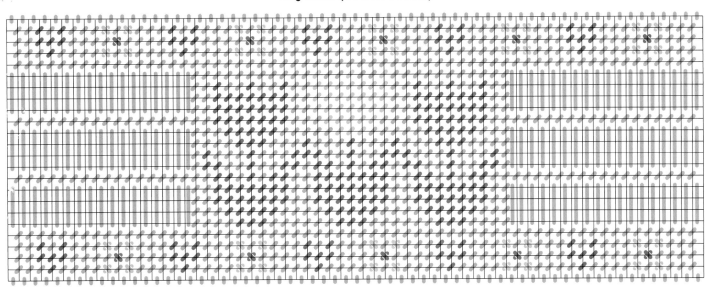

ULIP BASKET

(Shown on page 11)

Size: 5½"w x 4¾"h x 5½"d

Supplies: Worsted weight yarn, two 10½" x 13½" sheets of clear 7 mesh stiff plastic canvas, and #16 tapestry needle

Stitches Used: Gobelin Stitch, Overcast Stitch, and Tent Stitch

Instructions: Follow chart to cut and stitch Basket Side pieces. Cut a 38 x 38 piece of plastic canvas for Bottom. Bottom is not stitched.

Using green yarn, join Basket Sides together. Join Bottom to Basket Sides.

	COLOR	NL#
/	yellow	19
/	rose	05
/	green	53

Basket Side (38 x 32 threads) (stitch 4)

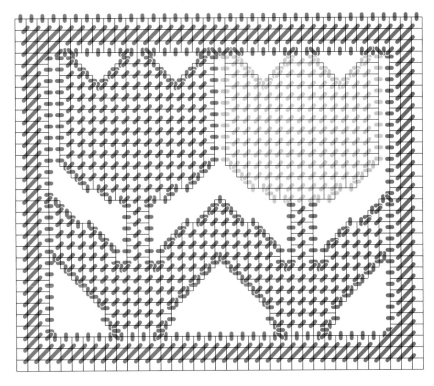

RUG

(Shown on page 12)

Size: 25"w x 16³/₄"h

Supplies: Worsted weight yarn, three 13¹/₂" x 21¹/₂" sheets of clear 5 mesh plastic canvas, #16 tapestry needle, nonskid rug backing (optional), and Scotchgard™ brand fabric protector

Stitches Used: Overcast Stitch, Scotch Stitch, and Tent Stitch

Instructions: Follow charts to cut and stitch Rug pieces, using two strands of yarn to work stitches. Complete background of each Rug section using ecru Tent Stitches as shown on charts.

Using dk green yarn, join Rug Section pieces together. Cover unworked edges of Rug.

If desired, follow manufacturer's instructions to apply fabric protector and nonskid rug backing to Rug.

Design by Kathleen Hurley.

BASKET TRIM

(Shown on page 13)

Size: 3"w x 3¹/₄"h

Supplies: Worsted weight yarn, one 10¹/₂" x 13¹/₂" sheet of clear 7 mesh plastic canvas, #16 tapestry needle, basket, two 24" lengths of 1"w wire-edge ribbon, and craft glue

Stitches Used: Gobelin Stitch, Modified Eyelet Stitch, Overcast Stitch, and Tent Stitch

Instructions: Follow charts to cut and stitch Large Pansy pieces. Using yellow yarn, tack Pansy Front to Back. Glue Leaves to Pansy. Glue one ribbon length to basket. Tie remaining ribbon into a bow and trim ends. Glue bow to basket. Glue Pansy to bow.

Design by Dick Martin.

COLOR	
✎	ecru
✎	yellow
✎	gold
✎	lt rose
✎	rose
✎	dk rose
✎	vy dk rose
✎	lt purple
✎	purple
✎	dk purple
✎	green
✎	dk green
✎	black

Iris Rug Section

(42 x 42 threads) (stitch 3)

Large Pansy Front
(14 x 14 threads)

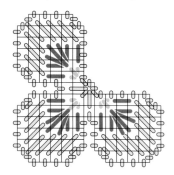

Large Pansy Leaf
(7 x 7 threads)
(stitch 2)

Large Pansy Back
(14 x 14 threads)

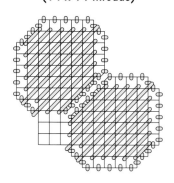

Pansy Rug Section
(42 x 42 threads) (stitch 3)

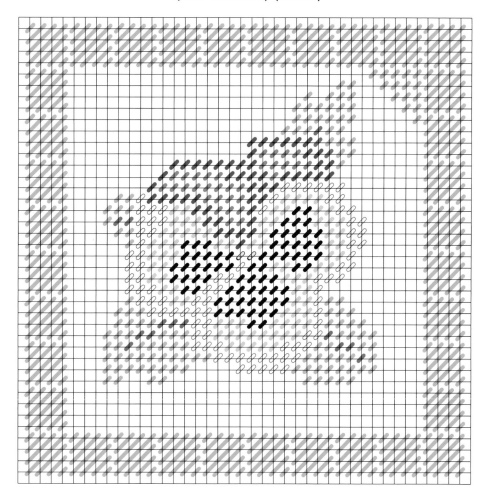

DAFFODIL

(Shown on page 13)

Size: 3½"w x 9"h

Supplies for One Daffodil: Worsted weight yarn, one 10½" x 13½" sheet of clear 7 mesh plastic canvas, #16 tapestry needle, six 18" lengths of #20 gauge floral wire, green floral tape, artificial greenery, 18" length of 1"w wire-edge ribbon, and green floral tape

Stitches Used: Gobelin Stitch, Overcast Stitch, and Tent Stitch

Instructions: Follow chart to cut and stitch Center, leaving stitches in blue shaded areas unworked. Matching ▲'s, overlap canvas and work stitches in blue shaded areas through both thicknesses of plastic canvas to join ends of Center, forming a cylinder. Using matching color yarn, join unworked edges of Center together, forming a bugle shape.

Follow chart to cut Petal pieces. For each Petal, bend one length of wire in half. Place wire along placement line on wrong side of Petal. Stitch Petal, covering wire as you work. Wrap wires with floral tape. Arrange Petals and wrap covered wires with floral tape to form flower stem. Using yarn color to match Center, tack Center to Petals.

Insert Daffodils and greenery into vase. Tie ribbon into a bow around vase and trim ends.

IRIS TISSUE BOX COVER

(Shown on page 13)

Size: 4½"w x 5¾"h x 4½"d

(Fits a 4¼"w x 5¼"h x 4¼"d boutique tissue box.)

Supplies: Worsted weight yarn, two 10½" x 13½" sheets of clear 7 mesh plastic canvas, and #16 tapestry needle

Stitches Used: Gobelin Stitch, Overcast Stitch, Tent Stitch, and Wound Cross Stitch

Instructions: Follow charts to cut and stitch pieces. Complete backgrounds of Side pieces using ecru Tent Stitches as shown on chart. Using ecru yarn, join Side pieces together along long edges. Join Top to Sides.

Tissue box cover design by Kathleen Hurley.

COLOR	
⟋	ecru
⟋	yellow
⟋	purple
⟋	dk purple
⟋	green
⟋	dk green
⟋	desired color
●	ecru French Knot
'	wire placement

Daffodil Center

(24 x 10 threads)

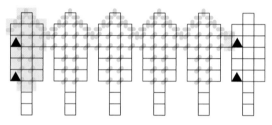

Daffodil Petal

(6 x 12 threads)

(stitch 6)

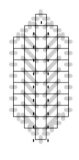

Tissue Box Cover Top

(32 x 32 threads)

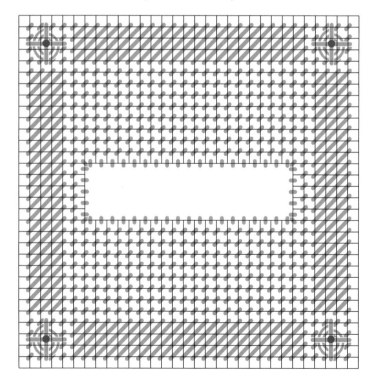

Tissue Box Cover Side

(32 x 38 threads) (stitch 4)

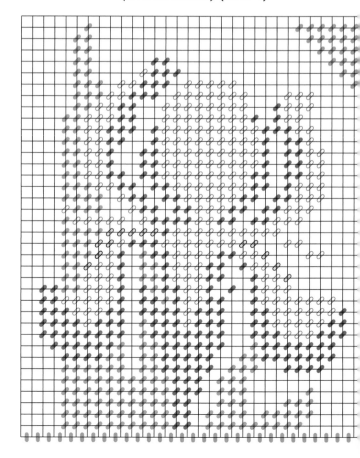

OTPOURRI BASKET

(Shown on page 13)

ize: 3¹/₂"w x 4¹/₄"h x 3¹/₄"d

upplies: Worsted weight yarn, one
0¹/₂" x 13¹/₂" sheet of clear 7 mesh
lastic canvas, #16 tapestry needle, and
raft glue

titches Used: Gobelin Stitch, Modified
yelet Stitch, Overcast Stitch, and Tent Stitch

struction: Follow charts to cut and stitch
mall Pansy and Basket pieces. Cut a
3 x 20 piece of plastic canvas for Basket
ottom. Basket Bottom is not stitched.
sing ecru yarn, join Basket Front to Sides.
oin Basket Back to Sides. Join Basket
ottom to Front, Back, and Sides. Tack
andle to Basket Front and Back.
sing rose yarn, tack Pansy Front to Back.
lue Leaves to Pansy. Glue Pansy to
asket Front.

Design by Dick Martin.

Basket Side
(20 x 17 threads) (stitch 2)

Basket Handle
(5 x 34 threads)

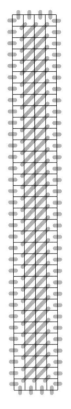

Basket Front/Back
(23 x 17 threads) (stitch 2)

COLOR	
⊘	ecru
⊘	yellow
⊘	lt rose
⊘	rose
⊘	dk rose
⊘	green
⊘	black

Small Pansy Back
(10 x 10 threads)

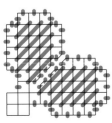

Small Pansy Leaves
(12 x 5 threads)

Small Pansy Front
(10 x 10 threads)

Pretty, yet practical

HEART COASTER SET

(Shown on page 14)

Holder Size: 4¹/₂"w x 5¹/₂"h x 3"d

Coaster Size: 4¹/₄"w x 4¹/₄"h

Supplies: Worsted weight yarn, two 10¹/₂" x 13¹/₂" sheets of clear 7 mesh plastic canvas, #16 tapestry needle, cork or felt (optional), and craft glue (optional)

Stitches Used: Backstitch, Cross Stitch, Gobelin Stitch, and Overcast Stitch

Instructions: Follow charts to cut and stitch pieces. Cut a 28 x 19 thread piece of plastic canvas for Bottom. Bottom is not stitched.

Using ecru yarn, join Front to Bottom. Join Back to Bottom. Join Sides to Bottom. Join Front to Back along unworked top edges. Refer to photo for placement and thread a 12" length of ecru yarn through Front and Side #1 pieces. Tie yarn into a bow and trim ends. Repeat for remaining corners of Holder.

If backing is desired, cut cork or felt slightly smaller than Coaster; glue to back of Coaster.

Design by Heidi Rabine.

Side #1
(19 x 22 threads)

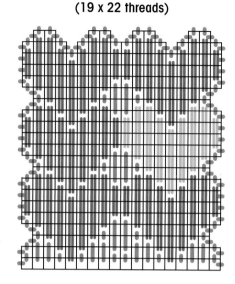

Side #2
(19 x 22 threads)

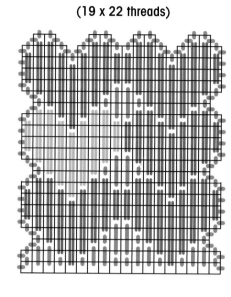

	COLOR
✐	ecru
✐	rose
✐	lt green
✐	green
✐	desired color

Front/Back
(28 x 40 threads)

Coaster
(29 x 29 threads) (stitch 4)

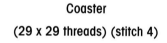

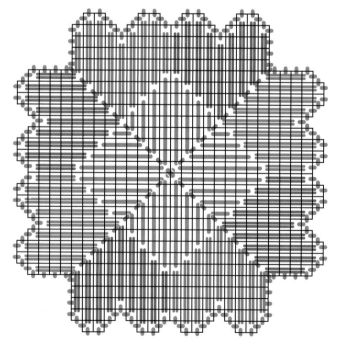

HEXAGON COASTER

(Shown on page 15)

Size: 5 1/2"w x 5"h

Supplies: Worsted weight yarn, 5" Uniek® hexagon plastic canvas piece, #16 tapestry needle, cork or felt (optional), and craft glue (optional)

Stitches Used: Backstitch, Gobelin Stitch, Overcast Stitch, and Tent Stitch

Instructions: Follow chart to cut and stitch design. Using dk blue yarn, cover unworked edges of Coaster. If backing is desired, cut cork or felt slightly smaller than Coaster; glue to back of Coaster.

Design by Ann Townsend.

FISH COASTER

(Shown on page 15)

Size: 4 1/4"w x 4"h

Supplies: Worsted weight yarn, one 10 1/2" x 13 1/2" sheet of clear 7 mesh plastic canvas, #16 tapestry needle, cork or felt (optional), and craft glue (optional)

Stitches Used: Backstitch, French Knot, Gobelin Stitch, Overcast Stitch, and Tent Stitch

Instructions: Follow chart to cut and stitch design. If backing is desired, cut cork or felt slightly smaller than Coaster; glue to back of Coaster.

Design by Dick Martin.

	COLOR	NL#
	lt blue	36
	blue	54
	dk blue	48

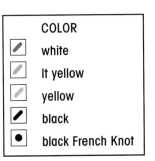

	COLOR
	white
	lt yellow
	yellow
	black
	black French Knot

Hexagon Coaster

Fish Coaster
(25 x 26 threads)

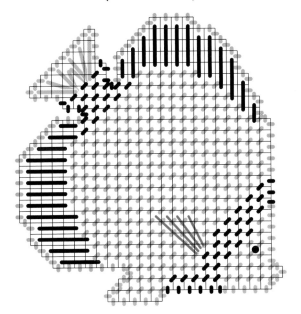

SAFARI COASTERS

(Shown on page 15)

Size: 6"w x 3½"h each

Supplies: Worsted weight yarn, one 10½" x 13½" sheet of clear 7 mesh plastic canvas, #16 tapestry needle, cork or felt (optional), and craft glue (optional)

Stitches Used: Fringe Stitch, Overcast Stitch, and Tent Stitch

Instructions: Follow charts to cut and stitch designs. Trim Fringe Stitches ¾" from knot. If backing is desired, cut cork or felt slightly smaller than Coaster; glue to back of Coaster.

	COLOR		COLOR
▱	white	▰	black
▱	gold	⊙	gold Fringe
▱	rust	⊙	black Fringe
▱	tan		

Zebra Coaster (29 x 24 threads)

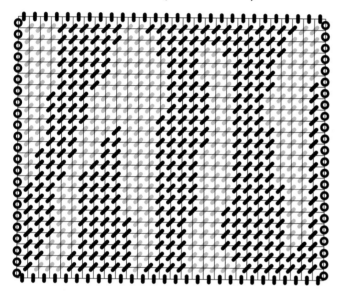

Tiger Coaster (29 x 24 threads)

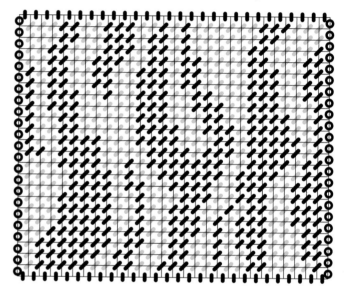

Giraffe Coaster (29 x 24 threads)

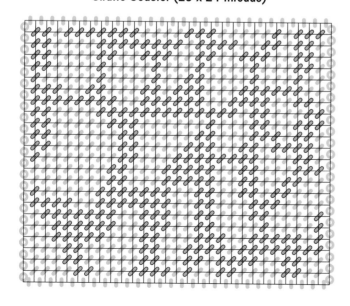

Leopard Coaster (29 x 24 threads)

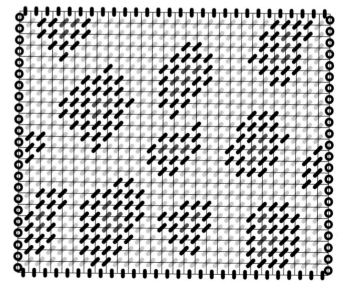

OME SWEET HOME BOOKEND

(hown on page 16)

ze: 4¹/₄"w x 8¹/₄"h x 2³/₄"d

pplies for One Bookend: Worsted weight yarn, two 10¹/₂" x 13¹/₂" eets of clear 7 mesh plastic canvas, #16 tapestry needle, /₂"w x 7¹/₂"h x 2¹/₈"d brick, and plastic wrap

itches Used: Backstitch, Gobelin Stitch, Overcast Stitch, and Tent tch

structions: Follow charts to cut and stitch pieces. Before adding ckstitches, complete background of Front with ecru Tent Stitches shown on chart. Cut a 28 x 55 thread piece of plastic canvas for ack. Cover Back with blue Gobelin Stitches as shown on Side chart. ut a 28 x 18 thread piece of plastic canvas for Bottom. Bottom is ot stitched.

sing blue yarn, join Front to Sides along long edges. Join Back to des. Join Top to Front, Back, and Sides.

rap brick with plastic wrap and insert brick into Bookend. Join ottom to Front, Back, and Sides.

esign by Ann Townsend.

Top (28 x 18 threads)

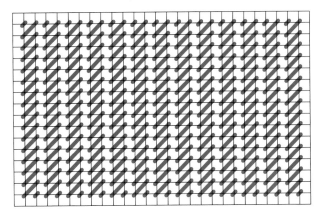

COLOR	
	ecru
	gold
	red
	blue
	green

Front (28 x 55 threads)

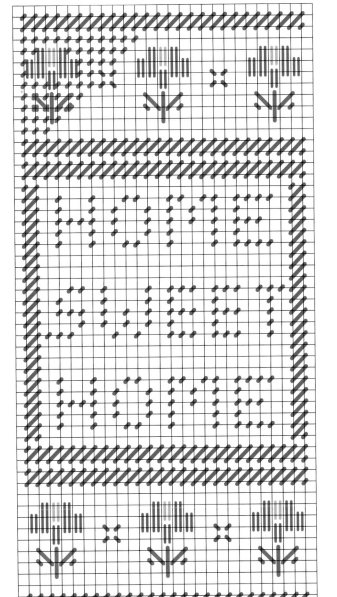

Side (18 x 55 threads) (stitch 2)

GEOMETRIC BOOKEND COVER

(Shown on page 17)

Size: 5¹/₂"w x 5³/₄"h x 2¹/₂"d

Supplies for One Bookend Cover: Worsted weight yarn, one 10¹/₂" x 13¹/₂" sheet of clear 7 mesh plastic canvas, #16 tapestry needle, and 4³/₄"w x 5"h metal bookend

Stitches Used: Byzantine Stitch, Gobelin Stitch, Milanese Stitch, Overcast Stitch, Scotch Stitch, and Tent Stitch

Instructions: Follow charts to cut and stitch pieces. Cut a 37 x 37 thread piece of plastic canvas for Back. Back is not stitched.

Using ecru yarn, join Front to Base between ▲'s. Join remaining unworked edges of Front to Back.

COLOR	
▱	ecru
▱	gold
▱	red
▰	blue
▱	green

Front (37 x 37 threads)

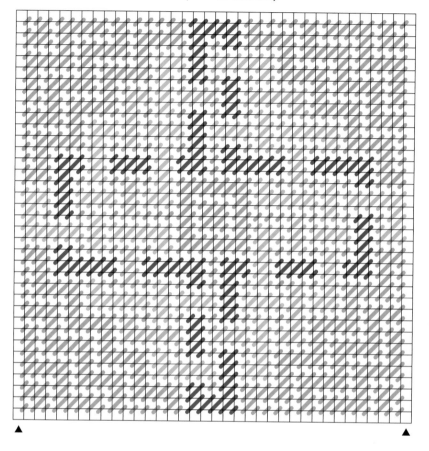

Base (37 x 15 threads)

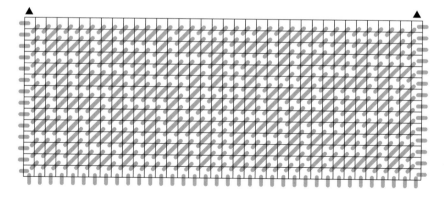

STRAWBERRY BASKET BOOKEND

(shown on page 17)

Size: 4¹/₄"w x 7³/₄"h x 2¹/₂"d

Supplies for One Bookend: Worsted weight yarn, two 10¹/₂" x 13¹/₂" sheets of clear 7 mesh plastic canvas, #16 tapestry needle, 7¹/₂"w x 7¹/₂"h x 2¹/₈"d brick, and plastic wrap

Stitches Used: Backstitch, French Knot, Gobelin Stitch, Mosaic Stitch, Overcast Stitch, and Tent Stitch

Instructions: Follow charts to cut and stitch pieces. Before adding backstitches, complete background of Front with ecru Tent Stitches as shown on chart. Cut a 28 x 52 thread piece of plastic canvas for Back. Cover Back with ecru Mosaic Stitches as shown on Side chart. Cut a 28 x 16 thread piece of plastic canvas for Bottom. Bottom is not stitched.

Referring to photo for yarn color, join Front to Sides along long edges. Using ecru yarn, join Back to Sides. Join Top to Front, Back, and Sides.

Wrap brick with plastic wrap and insert brick into Bookend. Using matching color yarn, join Bottom to Front, Back, and Sides.

Design by Kathleen Hurley.

Top (28 x 16 threads)

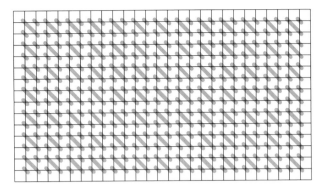

Front (28 x 52 threads)

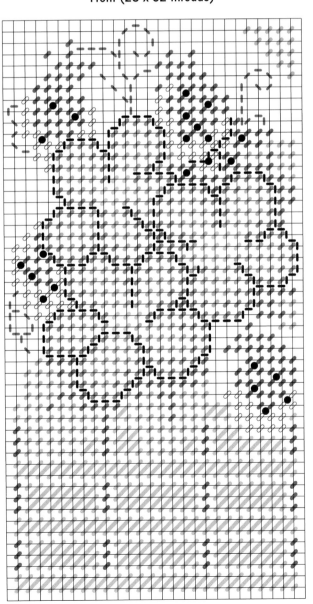

Side (16 x 52 threads) (stitch 2)

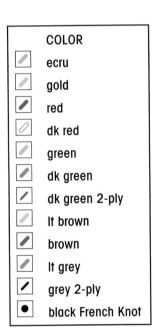

	COLOR
	ecru
	gold
	red
	dk red
	green
	dk green
	dk green 2-ply
	lt brown
	brown
	lt grey
	grey 2-ply
●	black French Knot

DIAMOND TISSUE BOX COVER

(Shown on page 18)

Size: 10"w x 3¹⁄₄"h x 5¹⁄₄"d
(Fits a 9¹⁄₂"w x 3"h x 4³⁄₄"d standard tissue box.)
Supplies: Worsted weight yarn, two 10¹⁄₂" x 13¹⁄₂" sheets of clear 7 mesh plastic canvas, and #16 tapestry needle
Stitches Used: Cross Stitch, Gobelin Stitch, Overcast Stitch, and Tent Stitch
Instructions: Follow charts to cut and stitch pieces. Using matching color yarn, join Top to Front along long edges. Join Back to Top. Join Top to Sides. Join Sides together.

Design by Esther Anderson.

COLOR	
✎	lt rose
✎	rose
✎	dk rose

Side (35 x 22 threads) (stitch 2)

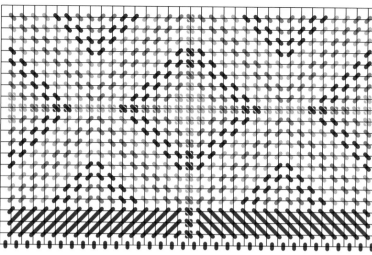

Front/Back (66 x 22 threads) (stitch 2)

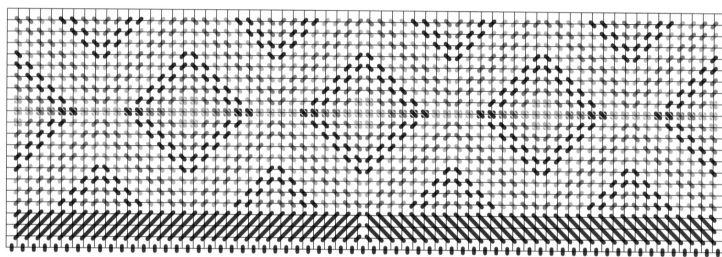

Top (66 x 35 threads)

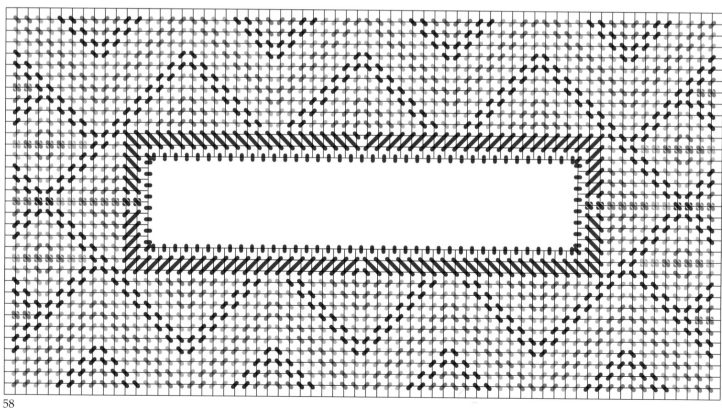

58

DELIGHTFUL PATTERN TISSUE BOX COVER

(Shown on page 19)

Size: 4¹/₂"w x 5³/₄"h x 4¹/₂"d
(Fits a 4¹/₄"w x 5¹/₄"h x 4¹/₄"d boutique tissue box.)

Supplies: Worsted weight yarn, two 10¹/₂" x 13¹/₂" sheets of clear 7 mesh plastic canvas, and #16 tapestry needle

Stitches Used: Braided Cross Stitch, Gobelin Stitch, Overcast Stitch, Shell Stitch, Smyrna Cross Stitch, Tent Stitch, and Waffle Stitch

Instructions: Follow charts to cut and stitch pieces. Using ecru Braided Cross Stitch, join Sides together along long edges. Join Top to Sides.

Design by Marcia Schorr.

Top (30 x 30 threads)

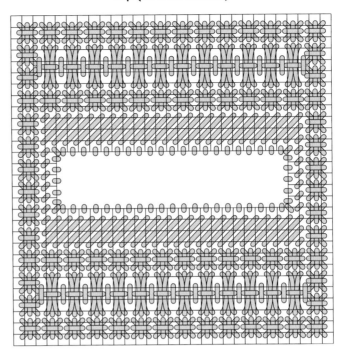

	COLOR
	ecru

Side (30 x 38 threads) (stitch 4)

SAFARI TISSUE BOX COVER

(Shown on page 19)

Size: 4³/₄"w x 5³/₄"h x 4³/₄"d
(Fits a 4¹/₄"w x 5¹/₄"h x 4¹/₄"d boutique tissue box.)

Supplies: Worsted weight yarn, two 10¹/₂" x 13¹/₂" sheets of clear 7 mesh plastic canvas, and #16 tapestry needle

Stitches Used: Backstitch, Gobelin Stitch, Overcast Stitch, and Tent Stitch

Instructions: Follow charts to cut and stitch pieces. Using brown yarn, join Sides together along long edges. Join Top to Sides.

Design by Conn Baker Gibney.

Top (32 x 32 threads)

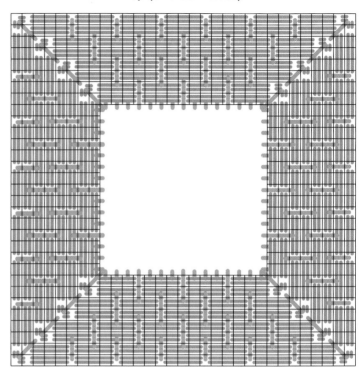

COLOR	
	beige
	tan
	brown
	black

Side #1 (32 x 38 threads) (stitch 2)

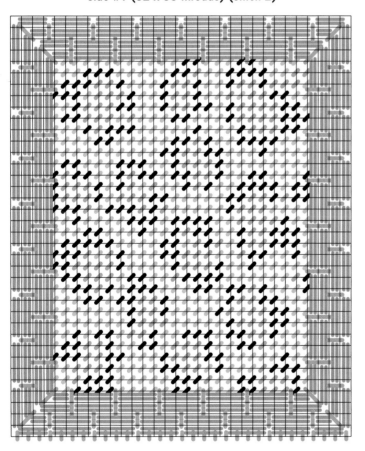

Side #2 (32 x 38 threads) (stitch 2)

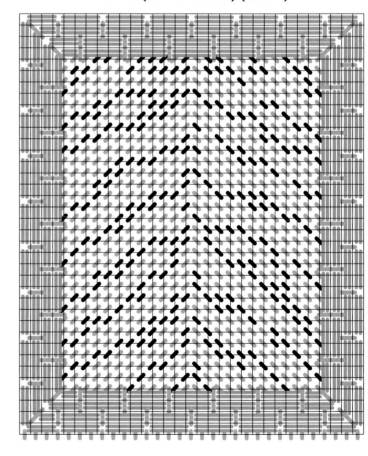

ORSE TISSUE BOX COVER

(Shown on page 19)

Size: 4³/₄"w x 5³/₄"h x 4³/₄"d

(Fits a 4¹/₄"w x 5¹/₄"h x 4¹/₄"d boutique tissue box.)

Supplies: Worsted weight yarn, silver metallic braid, dk brown DMC Embroidery Floss #938, two 10¹/₂" x 13¹/₂" sheets of clear 7 mesh plastic canvas, and #16 tapestry needle

Stitches Used: Backstitch, French Knot, Fringe Stitch, Overcast Stitch, and Tent Stitch

Instructions: Follow charts to cut and stitch pieces. Referring to photo, trim Fringe and separate plies to form mane on Front and Back. Using silver metallic yarn, add loops to bridle. Using green yarn, join Front to Sides along long edges. Join Back to Sides. Join Top to Front, Back, and Sides.

Design by Conn Baker Gibney.

	COLOR		COLOR
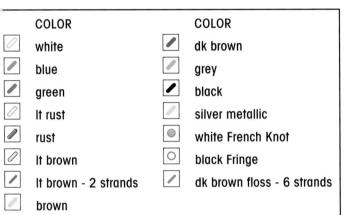	white		dk brown
	blue		grey
	green		black
	lt rust		silver metallic
	rust		white French Knot
	lt brown		black Fringe
	lt brown - 2 strands		dk brown floss - 6 strands
	brown		

Top (32 x 32 threads)

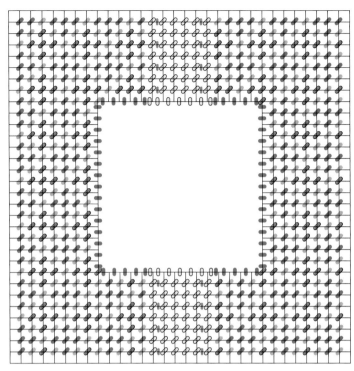

Front/Back (32 x 38 threads) (stitch 2)

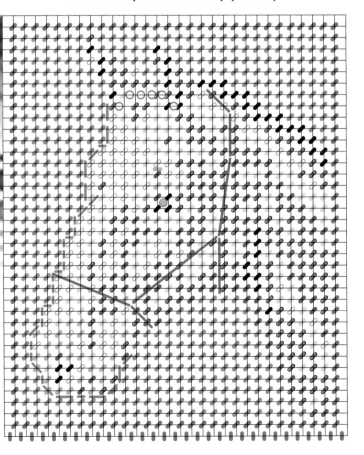

Side (32 x 38 threads) (stitch 2)

BIRDHOUSE TISSUE BOX COVER

(Shown on page 19)

Size: 4³/₄"w x 5¹/₂"h x 4³/₄"d
(Fits a 4¹/₄"w x 5¹/₄"h x 4¹/₄"d boutique tissue box.)

Supplies: Worsted weight yarn, black DMC Embroidery Floss #310, two 10¹/₂" x 13¹/₂" sheets of clear 7 mesh plastic canvas, and #16 tapestry needle

Stitches Used: Backstitch, French Knot, Overcast Stitch, and Tent Stitch

Instructions: Follow charts to cut and stitch pieces. Using matching color yarn, join Sides together along long edges. Using blue yarn, join Top to Sides.

Design by Michele Wilcox.

	COLOR	NL#	DMC#
⊘	yellow	57	
⊘	gold	17	
⊘	orange	12	
⊘	dk pink	55	
⊘	rose	06	
⊘	lavender	45	
⊘	lt blue	36	
⊘	blue	35	
⊘	grey blue	34	
⊘	green	28	
⊘	brown	13	
⊘	black	00	
⟋	black floss - 3 strands		310
●	black floss French Knot - 6 strands		310

Top (31 x 31 threads)

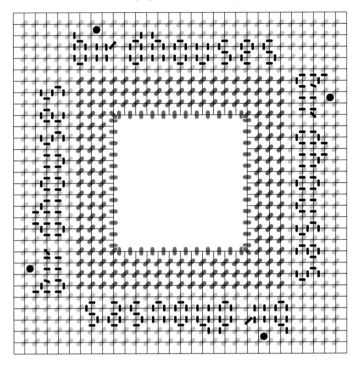

Side (31 x 37 threads) (stitch 4)

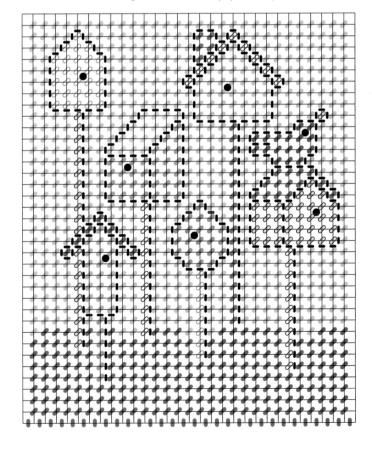

Hold everything!

FLORAL BASKET

(Shown on page 21)

Size: 8"w x 11"h x 8"d

Supplies: Worsted weight yarn, three 10½" x 13½" sheets of clear 7 mesh stiff plastic canvas, and #16 tapestry needle

Stitches Used: Cross Stitch, Overcast Stitch, and Tent Stitch

Instructions: Follow charts to cut and stitch pieces, leaving stitches in blue shaded area unworked. Using dk rose yarn, stitch initials with bottom of letters centered above purple dots on Side chart. Complete background of

Side pieces with ecru Tent Stitches as shown on chart.

Cut a 53 x 53 thread piece of plastic canvas for Bottom. Bottom is not stitched.

Overlap blue shaded areas on Handle pieces and work ecru Tent Stitches through both thicknesses of plastic canvas. Complete background of Handle with ecru Tent Stitches. Using green yarn, cover unworked edges of Handle.

Referring to photo for yarn color, join Side pieces together along short edges. Using ecru yarn, join Bottom to Sides. Using green yarn, tack Handle to Basket.

Design by Deborah Lambein.

COLOR	
	ecru
	yellow
	rose
	dk rose
	lavender
	blue
	green

Handle
(9 x 52 threads) (stitch 2)

Side (53 x 35 threads) (stitch 4)

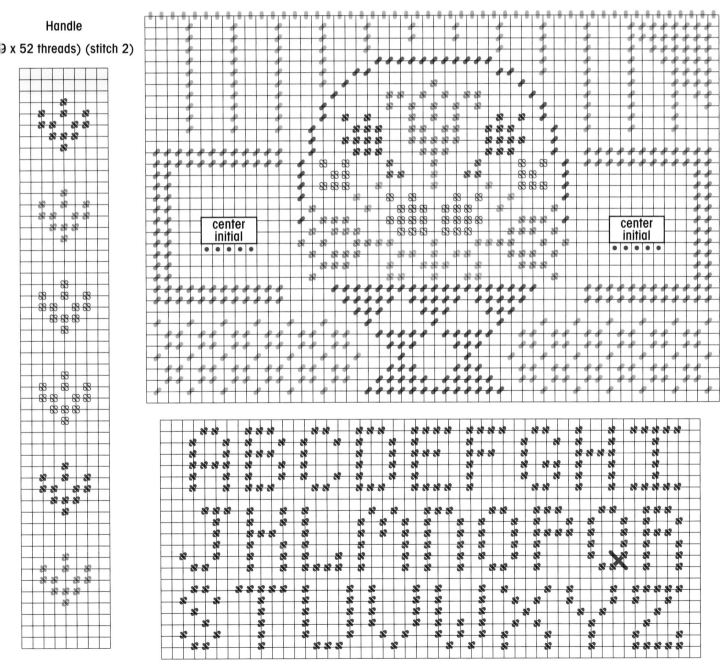

center
initial

center
initial

MINIATURE BASKET

(Shown on page 20)

Size: 4³/₄"h x 2¹/₂" dia.

Supplies: Worsted weight yarn, one 10¹/₂" x 13¹/₂" sheet of clear 7 mesh plastic canvas, 3" dia. Uniek® plastic canvas circle, and #16 tapestry needle

Stitches Used: Gobelin Stitch, Overcast Stitch, and Tent Stitch

Instructions: Follow charts to cut and stitch pieces. Refer to chart to cut Basket Bottom from plastic canvas circle along blue cutting line.

Using ecru yarn, join Basket Side together along short edges to form a cylinder. Using green yarn, join Basket Trim together along short edges. Join Basket Trim to Side.

Using ecru yarn, join Basket Bottom to Basket. Using green yarn, tack Handle to Basket.

Design by Ann Townsend.

NOTIONS BOX

(Shown on page 20)

Size: 12¹/₂"w x 4¹/₄"h x 4¹/₄"d

Supplies: Worsted weight yarn, two 10¹/₂" x 13¹/₂" sheets of clear 7 mesh stiff plastic canvas, and #16 tapestry needle

Stitches Used: Alternating Scotch Stitch, Backstitch, French Knot, Gobelin Stitch, Overcast Stitch, and Tent Stitch

Instructions: Follow charts to cut and stitch pieces. Cut a 84 x 28 thread piece of plastic canvas for Bottom. Bottom is not stitched. Using lt pink yarn, join Front to Sides. Join Back to Sides. Join Bottom to Front, Back, and Sides.

Design by Kooler Design Studio.

Notions Box Side (28 x 28 threads) (stitch 2)

Basket Bottom

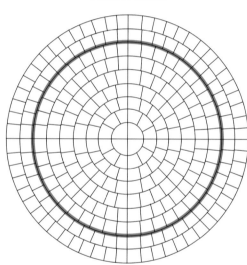

Basket Handle

(4 x 40 threads)

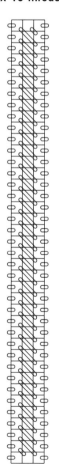

	COLOR				
	ecru		dk pink 2-ply		lt green
	yellow		purple		green
	lt pink		lt blue		green 2-ply
	pink		blue	●	blue 2-ply French Knot
	dk pink		blue 2-ply		

Basket Trim (54 x 6 threads)

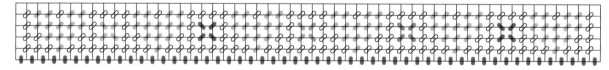

Basket Side (50 x 16 threads)

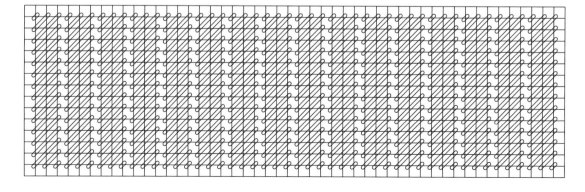

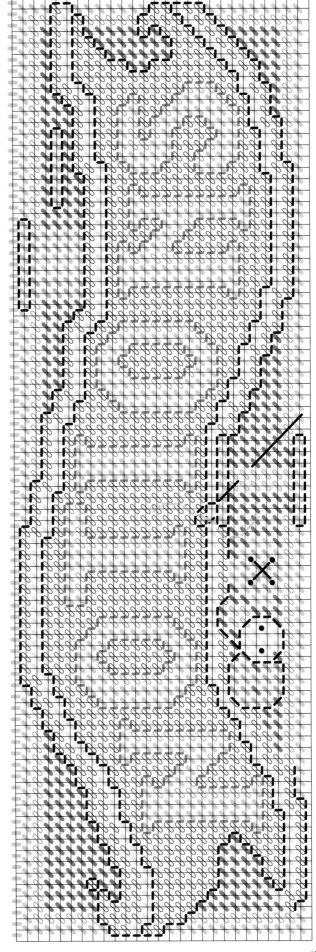

Notions Box Front (84 x 28 threads)

HEART BOX

(Shown on page 21)

Size: 6³/₄"w x 6"h x 2¹/₂"d

Supplies: Worsted weight yarn, one 10¹/₂" x 13¹/₂" sheet of clear 7 mesh plastic canvas, two 6" Uniek® heart plastic canvas pieces, and #16 tapestry needle

Stitches Used: Alternating Scotch Stitch, Backstitch, Gobelin Stitch, Overcast Stitch, and Tent Stitch

Instructions: Follow charts to cut and stitch pieces. Refer to chart to cut Bottom from one plastic canvas heart along blue cutting line.

Using ecru yarn, join Top Side pieces together along short edges. Join Top Sides to Top.

Join Bottom Side pieces together along short edges. Join Bottom Sides to Bottom.

Design by Pam Bull.

COLOR
ecru
pink
burgundy
blue

Top

Bottom

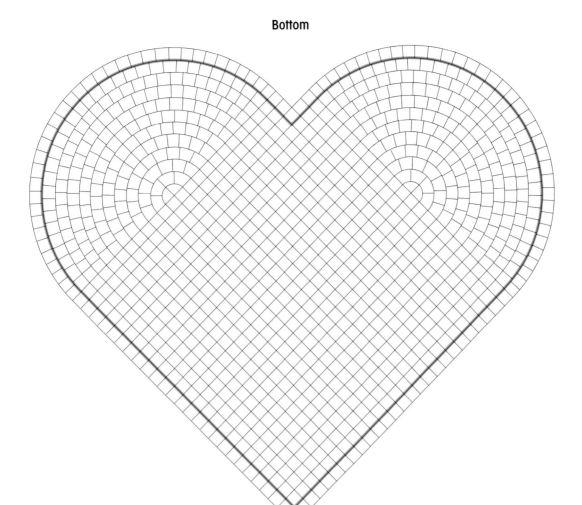

Top Side (67 x 6 threads) (stitch 2)

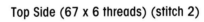
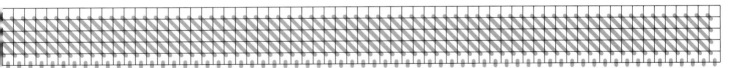

Bottom Side (63 x 16 threads) (stitch 2)

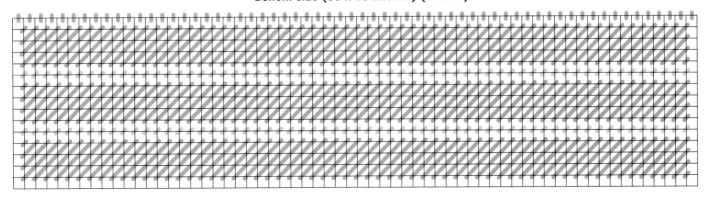

Unexpected touches

HEART WALL HANGING

(Shown on page 22)

Size: 6³/₄"w x 6"h

Supplies: Worsted weight yarn, one 10¹/₂" x 13¹/₂" sheet of clear 7 mesh plastic canvas, 6" Uniek® heart plastic canvas piece, #16 tapestry needle, sawtooth hanger, and craft glue

Stitches Used: Backstitch, Overcast Stitch, and Tent Stitch

Instructions: Refer to chart to cut Border from plastic canvas heart along blue cutting line. Follow charts to cut and stitch pieces. Using red yarn, cover unworked edges of Border.

Glue Border to Center. Glue sawtooth hanger to back of Heart.

Design by Michele Wilcox.

Center
(40 x 33 threads)

COLOR	
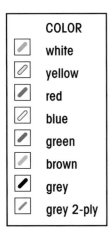	white
	yellow
	red
	blue
	green
	brown
	grey
	grey 2-ply

Border

LADYBUG PLANT POKE

(Shown on page 22)

Size: 1³/₄"w x 1"h x 2"d

Supplies: Worsted weight yarn, black DMC embroidery Floss #310, one 10¹/₂" x 13¹/₂" sheet of clear 7 mesh plastic canvas, #16 tapestry needle, 10" wooden skewer, two 7mm moving eyes, two 1¹/₄" lengths of black chenille stem, and craft glue

Stitches Used: Backstitch, Overcast Stitch, and Tent Stitch

Instructions: Follow charts to cut and stitch pieces. Using matching color yarn, fold and join inside edges of Top as indicated by arrows. Using matching color yarn, join Top to Bottom. For antennae, insert chenille stems through canvas at ▲'s; glue in place. Glue eyes to Ladybug.

Design by Terry A. Ricioli.

LOOSE CHANGE BANK

(Shown on page 23)

Size: 6¹/₂"w x 3¹/₂"h x 1¹/₂"d

Supplies: Worsted weight yarn, one 10¹/₂" x 13¹/₂" sheet of clear 7 mesh plastic canvas, and #16 tapestry needle

Stitches Used: Gobelin Stitch, Overcast Stitch, and Tent Stitch

Instructions: Follow charts to cut and stitch pieces. Using white yarn, join Bank Front to Sides. Join Back to Sides. Join Top to Sides.

For Bottom, cut two pieces of plastic canvas 11 x 24 threads each. Bottom is not stitched. Overlap short edges of Bottom pieces five threads and tack together. Join Bottom pieces to Front, Back, and Sides. To remove coins from Bank, cut yarn used to tack Bottom together and squeeze Bank Sides to separate Bottom pieces.

Design by Mary Billeaudeau.

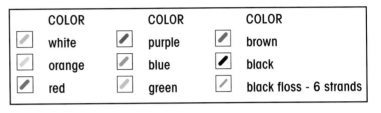

COLOR	COLOR	COLOR
white	purple	brown
orange	blue	black
red	green	black floss - 6 strands

Ladybug Top

(19 x 19 threads)

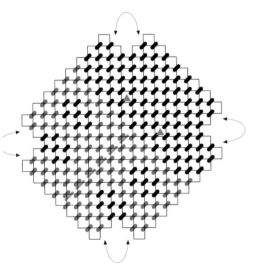

Ladybug Bottom

(15 x 15 threads)

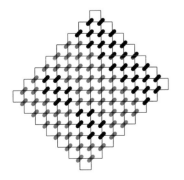

Bank Side

(23 x 11 threads) (stitch 2)

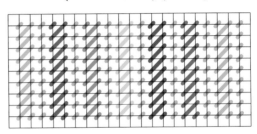

Bank Top

(43 x 11 threads)

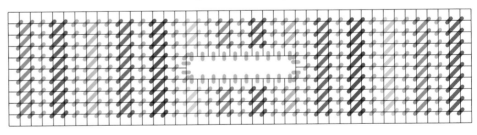

Bank Front/Back

(43 x 23 threads) (stitch 2)

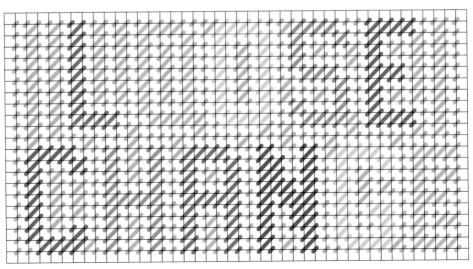

POTPOURRI BOTTLE

(Shown on page 23)

Size: 10³/₄"h x 2" dia.

Supplies: Worsted weight yarn, one 10¹/₂" x 13¹/₂" sheet of clear 7 mesh plastic canvas, #16 tapestry needle, ³/₄" dia. piece of cork, potpourri, and craft glue

Stitches Used: Gobelin Stitch, Overcast Stitch, and Tent Stitch

Instructions: Follow charts to cut and stitch pieces. Using purple yarn, join Bottle edges together between ■'s and ★'s. Fold and join inside edges of Bottle together as indicated by arrows. Insert cork into top of Bottle. Fill Bottle with potpourri. Join Bottom to Bottle.

Design by Becky Dill.

COLOR	
✏	purple

Bottle Bottom

(12 x 12 threads)

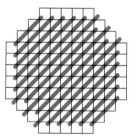

Bottle

(40 x 71 threads)

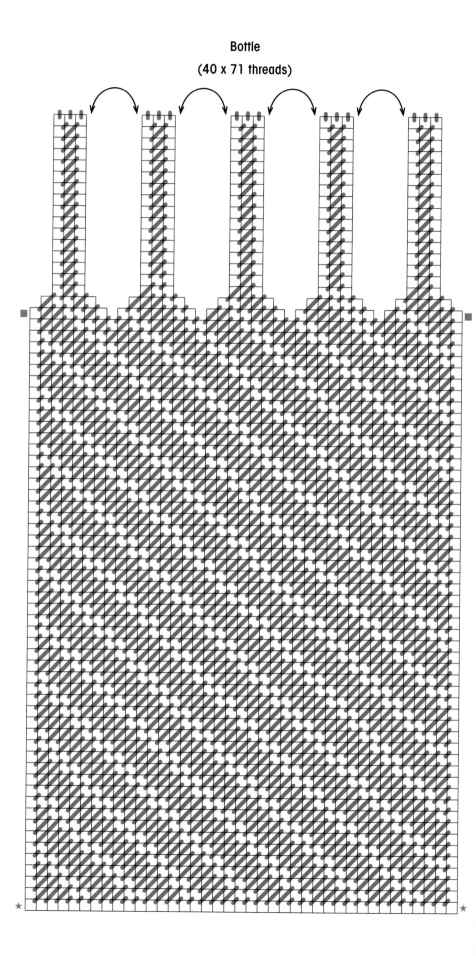

70

GER LILY CANDLE HOLDER

(shown on page 23)

ze: 3¹/₄"w x 8¹/₄"h x 3¹/₄"d

upplies: Worsted weight yarn, one
0¹/₂" x 13¹/₂" sheet of clear 7 mesh plastic
anvas, #16 tapestry needle, eight 10"
ngths of 20 gauge floral wire, and
ooden skewer

itches Used: Backstitch, Diagonal Leaf
itch, Gobelin Stitch, Overcast Stitch, and
nt Stitch

structions: Follow charts to cut pieces.
itch Base through both thicknesses of
astic canvas. Using green yarn, cover
nworked edges of Base.
old one length of floral wire in half. Place
oral wire on back of one Flower Section
long wire placement line. Follow chart to
itch Flower Section, covering wire as you
itch. Repeat for remaining Flower Section
ieces. Using green yarn, join unworked
dges of Flower Sections together to form a
ylinder. Tack Flower to Base. Refer to
hoto to bend petals in place.
itch Bee pieces. Using white yarn, tack
ne Wing to each Bee piece. Using yellow
arn, join one Bee Side #1 to Side #2.
epeat for remaining Bee pieces.
ind one piece of wire tightly around
kewer; remove wire from skewer. Hook
nds of wire to one Bee piece and Flower.
epeat to attach remaining Bee to Flower.

Design by Becky Dill.

	COLOR
	white
	yellow
	orange
	green
	black
	black 2-ply
I	wire placement

Bee Side #1

(7 x 5 threads)

(stitch 2)

Bee Side #2

(7 x 5 threads)

(stitch 2)

Bee Wing

(4 x 5 threads)

(stitch 4)

Flower Section

(6 x 62 threads)

(stitch 6)

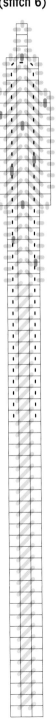

Base

(22 x 22 threads) (cut 2)

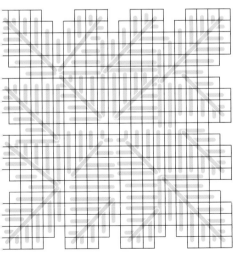

POTPOURRI CUBES

(Shown on page 24)

Size: 2"w x 2"h x 2"d

Supplies for One Cube: Worsted weight yarn, one 10¹/₂" x 13¹/₂" sheet of white 7 mesh plastic canvas, and #16 tapestry needle, 8" length of ¹/₈"w white satin ribbon, and potpourri

Stitches Used: Backstitch, Gobelin Stitch, Mosaic Stitch, Overcast Stitch, and Tent Stitch

Instructions: Follow charts to cut and stitch Side pieces to make desired Cube. Cut two pieces of plastic canvas 14 x 14 threads each for Top and Bottom. Top and Bottom are not stitched.

Using blue yarn, join Sides together to form a box. Join Bottom to Sides. Fill cube with potpourri. For hanger, fold ribbon length in half. Thread loose ends of ribbon through center of Top. Secure loose ends on wrong side of Top with a knot. Join Top to Sides.

Designs by Ann Townsend.

HOUSE SUGAR PACKET HOLDER

(Shown on page 24)

Size: 3¹/₂"w x 2³/₄"h x 2¹/₂"d

Supplies: Worsted weight yarn, one 10¹/₂" x 13¹/₂" sheet of white 7 mesh plastic canvas, and #16 tapestry needle

Stitches Used: Backstitch, Cross Stitch, French Knot, Gobelin Stitch, Overcast Stitch, and Tent Stitch

Instructions: Follow charts to cut and stitch House and Roof pieces. Cut a 19 x 12 thread piece of plastic canvas for Bottom. Bottom is not stitched.

Using dk blue yarn, join Roof Front to Back along long unworked edges. Join Front to one Side piece between ▲'s. Join remaining unworked edges of Sides to Front and Back.

Using white yarn, join House Front to Sides. Join Back to Sides. Join Bottom to Front, Back, and Sides.

Design by Dixie Lee Scoby.

Potpourri Cube #1 Side
(14 x 14 threads) (stitch 4)

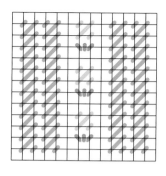

Potpourri Cube #2 Side
(14 x 14 threads) (stitch 4)

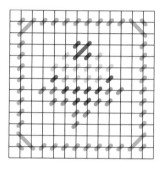

Roof Side
(12 x 12 threads) (stitch 2)

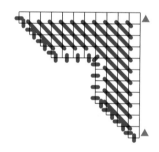

Roof Front/Back
(22 x 12 threads)

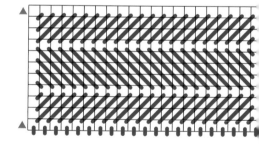

COLOR	
	white
pink	
dk pink	
blue	
dk blue	
green	
●	white French Knot

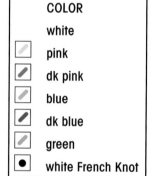

House Front
(19 x 12 threads)

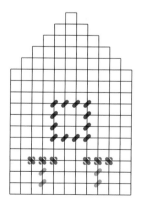

House Side
(12 x 17 threads) (stitch 2)

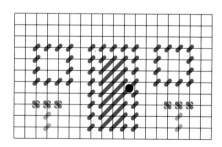

House Back
(19 x 12 threads)

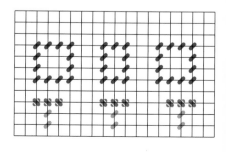

NAPKIN RINGS

(Shown on page 24)

Size: 1³/₄" dia.

Supplies for One Napkin Ring: Worsted weight yarn, one 10¹/₂" x 13¹/₂" sheet of white 7 mesh plastic canvas, and #16 tapestry needle

Stitches Used: Cross Stitch, Overcast Stitch, and Tent Stitch

Instructions: Follow charts to cut and stitch design to make desired Napkin Ring. Using matching color yarn, join unworked edges of plastic canvas together to form a cylinder.

Designs by Ann Townsend.

NOTEPAD HOLDER

(Shown on page 25)

Size: 4¹/₂"w x 1"h x 6¹/₂"d

Supplies: Worsted weight yarn, one 10¹/₂" x 13¹/₂" sheet of clear 7 mesh plastic canvas, #16 tapestry needle, 12" square of blue felt, and craft glue

Stitches Used: Mosaic Stitch and Overcast Stitch

Instructions: Follow charts to cut and stitch pieces, leaving stitches in yellow shaded areas unworked. Cut a 30 x 44 thread piece of plastic canvas for Bottom. Bottom is not stitched.

Cut lining pieces from felt using plastic canvas pieces as patterns. Do not line pencil holder portion of Back.

Using lt blue yarn, match ✳'s and work stitches in yellow shaded area to form pencil holder.

Join Front to Sides along short edges. Join Back to Sides. Join Front, Back, and Sides to Bottom. Glue felt pieces to Notepad Holder.

COLOR	
	white
	yellow
	pink
	dk pink
	lavender
	purple
	lt blue
	dk blue
	green

Napkin Ring #1
(33 x 11 threads)

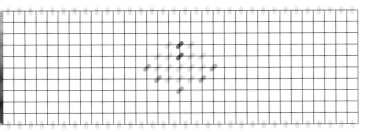

Napkin Ring #2
(33 x 11 threads)

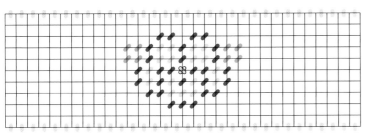

Notepad Holder Front
(30 x 8 threads)

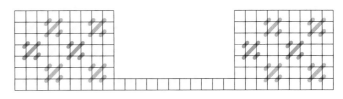

Notepad Holder Back
(30 x 19 threads)

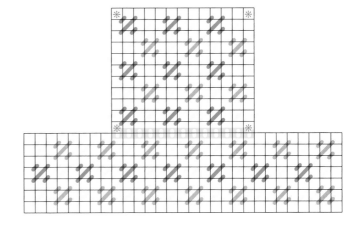

Notepad Holder Side
(44 x 8 threads) (stitch 2)

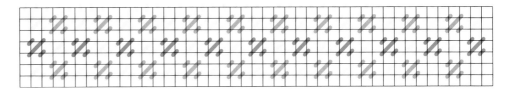

BASKET BORDERS

(Shown on page 25)

Size: 13¹/₂" dia. each

Supplies for One Basket: Sport weight yarn, one 10¹/₂" x 13¹/₂" sheet of white 10 mesh plastic canvas, #16 tapestry needle, small basket 10¹/₂" - 12¹/₂" dia. at top of basket, 18" square of desired color fabric, 12" length of ⁵/₈"w grosgrain or satin ribbon to match fabric, polyester fiberfill, and craft glue

Stitches Used: Cross Stitch, Overcast Stitch, Scotch Stitch, and Tent Stitch

Instructions: Cut an 11 x 137 thread piece of plastic canvas. Follow chart to stitch design, repeating stitches to approximately

five threads from right edge of plastic canvas.

Glue approximately ¹/₂" layer of fiberfill to outside of basket. With wrong side facing upward, place basket in center of fabric square. Gather fabric around basket and fold ends around top edge of basket, cutting holes for handles if needed. Glue wrong side of fabric to inside top edge of basket and trim ends. Glue ribbon to inside top edge of basket to cover raw edges of fabric. Overlap ends of canvas and glue to back of fabric-covered basket.

Designs by Ann Townsend.

COLOR	
/	yellow
/	pink
/	dk pink
/	lavender
/	purple
/	blue
/	green

Basket Border #1

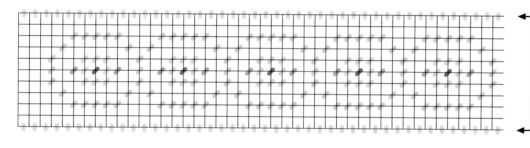

Continue stitching design to right edge of canvas.

Basket Border #2

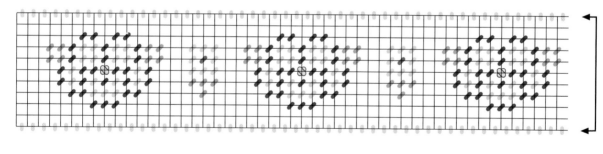

Continue stitching design to right edge of canvas.

Basket Border #3

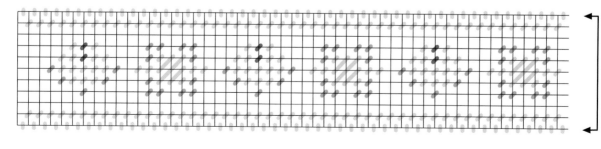

Continue stitching design to right edge of canvas.

PEAR PICTURE

(Shown on page 26)

Size: 5¼"w x 5¼"h

Supplies: DMC #3 Pearl Cotton (refer to color key), brown DMC Embroidery Floss #898, one 10½" x 13½" sheet of clear 10 mesh plastic canvas, #20 tapestry needle, and custom frame

Stitches Used: Backstitch, French Knot, and Tent Stitch

Instructions: Follow chart to cut and stitch design. Before adding Backstitches, complete background with beige Tent Stitches as indicated on chart. Insert stitched piece into custom frame.

Design by Michele Wilcox.

COLOR	DMC#		COLOR	DMC#
ecru			brown floss - 3 strands	898
yellow	745		brown floss French Knot - 6 strands	898
dk red	902			
yellow green	832			
green	911			
dk green	500			
beige	738			
brown	898			

Pear (53 x 53 threads)

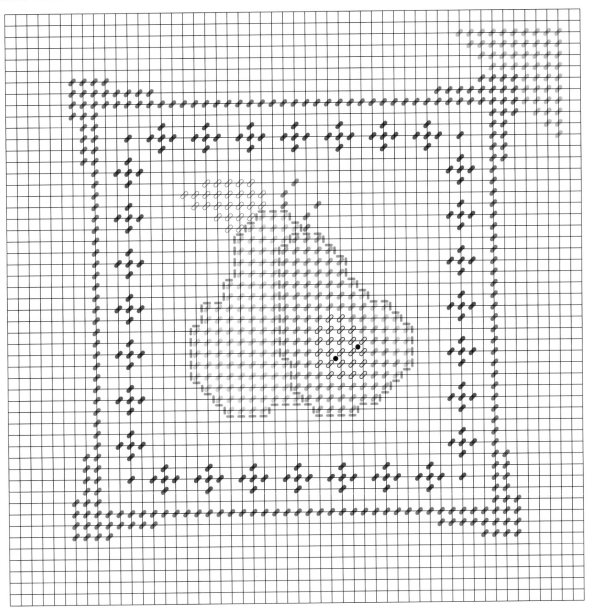

PADDED FRAME

(Shown on page 26)

Size: 6¹/₂"w x 8¹/₄"h
(Photo opening is 4¹/₄"w x 6"h.)

Supplies: Worsted weight yarn, one 10¹/₂" x 13¹/₂" sheet of clear 7 mesh stiff plastic canvas, #16 tapestry needle, 26" length of ¹/₂" dia. cord, sawtooth hanger, and craft glue

Stitches Used: Gobelin Stitch and Overcast Stitch

Instructions: Follow chart to cut and stitch Frame Front, leaving stitches in pink shaded area unworked. For complete coverage, work two gold Gobelin Stitches in each hole. Work three variegated stitches in each hole.

Place cord over shaded area overlapping ends; trim ends. Work stitches in pink shaded area to cover cord.

Cut a piece of plastic canvas 44 x 55 threads for Back. Back is not stitched. Using gold straight Gobelin stitches over three threads, join Front to Back along unworked edges of Front.

Glue sawtooth hanger to back of Frame.

Design by Ruby Thacker.

COLOR	NL#
gold	17
variegated	

Front (44 x 55 threads)

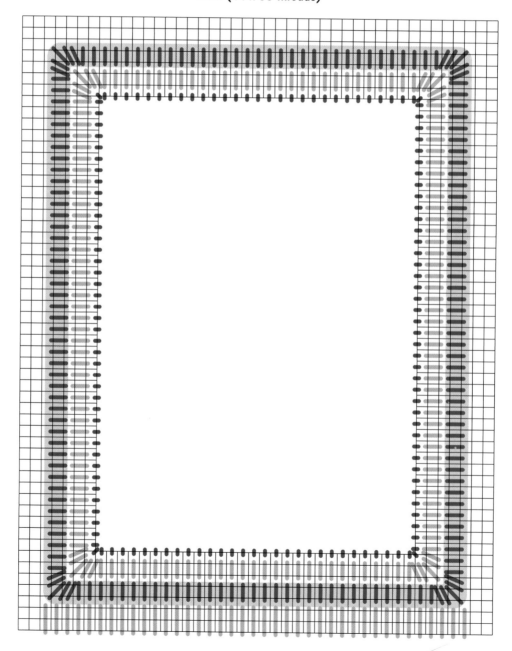

76

SQUARE CLOCK

(Shown on page 27)

Size: 6¼"w x 6¼"h x 1"d

Supplies: Worsted weight yarn, one 10½" x 13½" sheet of clear 7 mesh stiff plastic canvas, #16 tapestry needle, and battery operated clock movement for ¼" thick clock face

Stitches Used: Cross Stitch, French Knot, Gobelin Stitch, Oriental Stitch, Overcast Stitch, and Tent Stitch

Instructions: Follow charts to cut and stitch pieces. Before adding French Knots, complete background of Front with beige Tent Stitches as indicated on chart.

Using gold yarn, join Sides to Front. Join Sides together along short edges.

Insert clock movement shaft through hole in Front. Follow manufacturer's instructions to assemble clock hands. Join Back to Sides.

	COLOR	NL#
	gold	17
	beige	40
	gold French Knot	17

Side (7 x 42 threads) (stitch 4)

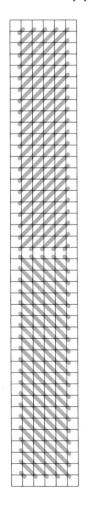

Front (42 x 42 threads)

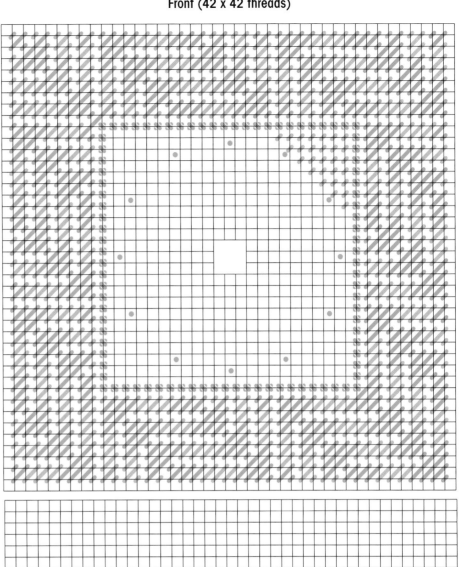

Back (42 x 42 threads)

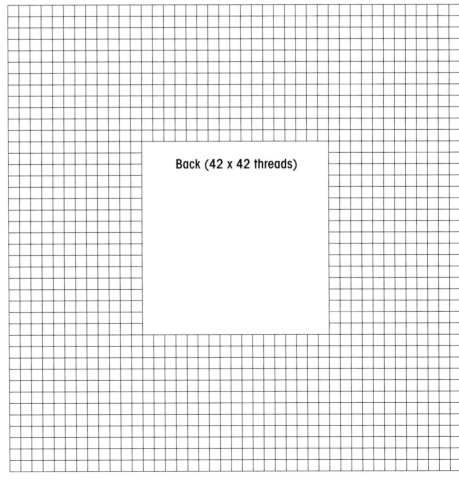

SAMPLER

(Shown on page 27)

Size: 9³/₄"w x 9³/₄"h

Supplies: Worsted weight yarn, one 10¹/₂" x 13¹/₂" sheet of clear 7 mesh plastic canvas, #16 tapestry needle, and custom frame

Stitches Used: Alicia Lace Stitch, Alternating Scotch Stitch, Boxed Scotch Stitch, Checked Scotch Stitch, Condensed Cashmere Stitch, Diagonal Couching Stitch, Flat Stitch, Gobelin Stitch, Jacquard Stitch, Milanese Stitch, Modified Jacquard Stitch, Oriental Stitch, Smyrna Cross Stitch, Tent Stitch, and Upright Cross Stitch

Instructions: Follow chart to cut and stitch design. Insert stitched piece into custom frame.

Design by Diane W. Villano.

	COLOR	NL#
	gold	17
	beige	40
	beige	40

Sampler (66 x 66 threads)

Oaby talk

DOORKNOB HANGER

(Shown on page 28)

Size: 4"w x 11½"h

Supplies: Worsted weight yarn, one 10½" x 13½" sheet of clear 7 mesh plastic canvas, and #16 tapestry needle

Stitches Used: Gobelin Stitch, Mosaic Stitch, Overcast Stitch, and Tent Stitch

Instructions: Follow chart to cut and stitch design. Using white yarn, cover unworked edges of Doorknob Hanger.

Design by Kooler Design Studio, Inc.

KOOLER DESIGN STUDIO

COLOR	
	white
	yellow
	peach
	pink
	blue
	green

Doorknob Hanger

(26 x 76 threads)

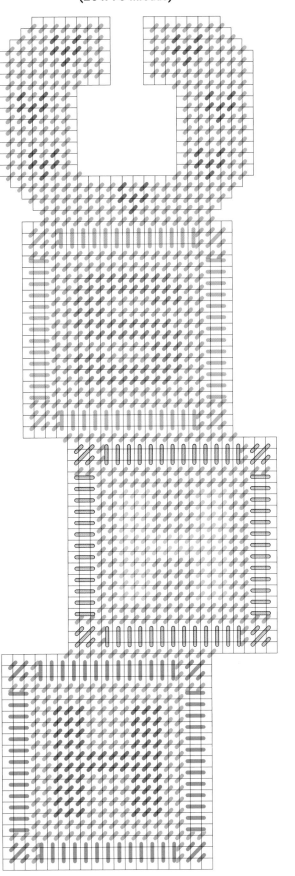

BABY FRAME

(Shown on page 28)

Size: 11³/₄"w x 9"h x 2¹/₂"d
(Photo opening is 6"w x 4¹/₂"h.)

Supplies: Worsted weight yarn, three 10¹/₂" x 13¹/₂" sheets of clear 7 mesh stiff plastic canvas, #16 tapestry needle, and craft glue

Stitches Used: Gobelin Stitch, Mosaic Stitch, Overcast Stitch, Scotch Stitch, and Tent Stitch

Instructions: Follow chart to cut and stitch Frame Front. Cut a piece of plastic canvas 71 x 59 threads for Frame Back. Cut a piece of plastic canvas 71 x 15 threads for Frame Bottom. Frame Back and Bottom are not stitched.

Using white yarn, join top edge of Frame Front to Back. Join remaining long edge of Frame Front to Bottom. Join Frame Back to Bottom.

Follow charts to cut and stitch B, A, B, and Y pieces. Using white yarn, cover unworked edges of stitched pieces. Refer to photo and glue B, A, B, and Y pieces to Frame.

BABY BLOCK

(Shown on page 29)

Size: 3"w x 3"h x 3"d

Supplies: Worsted weight yarn, on 10¹/₂" x 13¹/₂" sheet of clear 7 mesh plastic canvas, and #16 tapestry needle

Stitches Used: Gobelin Stitch, Mosaic Stitch, Overcast Stitch, and Tent Stitch

Instructions: For Sides, follow charts to cut and stitch B, A, B, and Y pieces. Cut and stitch Block Top and Bottom. Using white yarn, join Sides together to form a box. Join Top and Bottom to Sides.

Designs by Kooler Design Studio, Inc.

	COLOR
	white
	yellow
	peach
	pink
	blue
	green

B
(20 x 20 threads)

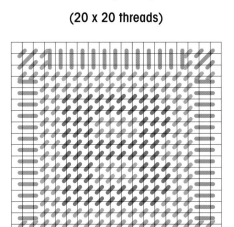

A
(20 x 20 threads)

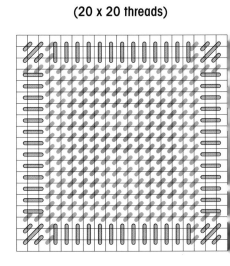

Block Top/Bottom
(20 x 20 threads)

B
(20 x 20 threads)

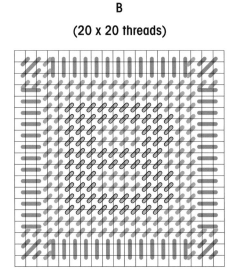

Y
(20 x 20 threads)

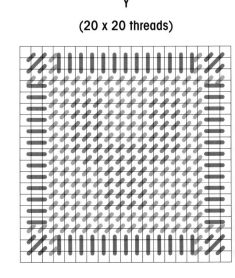

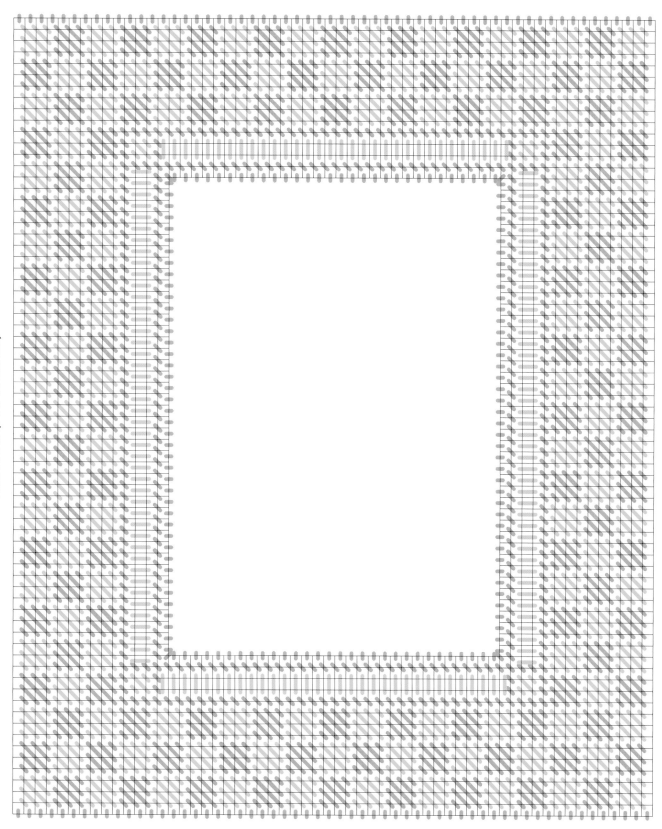

Frame Front (71 x 59 threads)

DIAPER BOX

(Shown on page 29)

Size: 6"w x 4¹/₂"h x 4¹/₂"d

Supplies: Worsted weight yarn, two 10¹/₂" x 13¹/₂" sheets of clear 7 mesh stiff plastic canvas, and #16 tapestry needle

Stitches Used: Backstitch, Gobelin Stitch, Overcast Stitch, Scotch Stitch, and Tent Stitch

Instructions: Follow charts to cut and stitch Diaper Box pieces. Cut a 40 x 30 thread piece of plastic canvas for Bottom. Bottom is not stitched. Using white yarn, join Front to Sides. Join Back to Sides. Join Bottom to Front, Back, and Sides.

HORSE

(Shown on page 29)

Size: 4¹/₂"w x 3³/₄"h x 1"d

Supplies: Worsted weight yarn, one 10¹/₂" x 13¹/₂" sheet of clear 7 mesh plastic canvas, and #16 tapestry needle

Stitches Used: Backstitch, Cross Stitch, Fringe Stitch, Overcast Stitch, and Tent Stitch

Instructions: Follow charts to cut and stitch Horse pieces, leaving pink shaded areas unworked. Match symbols to join pieces together as follows.

Using matching color yarn, join Rocker Ends to Rocker between ♦'s. Matching ✖'s, join Rocker and Rocker Ends to Horse Front and Back.

Using white yarn, join Front to Back between ✳'s, leaving pink shaded areas unworked. For mane, work Fringe Stitches in pink shaded area on Front through both thicknesses of plastic canvas. Separate plies of Fringe Stitches; trim ends.

Using pink yarn, join Saddle Top to Saddle Front and Back. Tack Saddle to Horse.

For tail, cut four 8" lengths of desired color yarn. Thread yarn through Horse Front and Back at ▲'s, keeping yarn ends even. Wrap a 6" length of matching color yarn around tail near ▲'s. Tie 6" yarn length into a knot around 8" lengths; trim all yarn ends.

BABY BANK

(Shown on page 29)

Size: 4¹/₂"w x 6³/₄"h x 3"d

Supplies: Worsted weight yarn, two 10¹/₂" x 13¹/₂" sheets of clear 7 mesh plastic canvas, #16 tapestry needle, and craft glue

Stitches Used: Backstitch, Cross Stitch, Fringe Stitch, Mosaic Stitch, Overcast Stitch, and Tent Stitch

Instructions: Follow charts to cut and stitch Bank pieces. Use white yarn for all joining and tacking. Join Bank Front to Sides. Join Back to Sides. Join Top to Front, Back, and Sides.

Cut two pieces of plastic canvas 20 x 18 threads each for Bottom. Bottom pieces are not stitched. Overlap long edges of Bottom pieces six threads and tack together. Join Bottom to Front, Back, and Sides.

Follow Horse instructions to cut, stitch, and assemble Horse. Glue Horse to Bank. To remove coins from Bank, remove yarn on overlapped area of Bottom and squeeze Bank.

Designs by Kooler Design Studio, Inc.

82

	COLOR			COLOR
	white			green
	yellow			desired color
	pink		○	desired color Fringe
	blue			

Diaper Box Side (30 x 30 threads) (stitch 2)

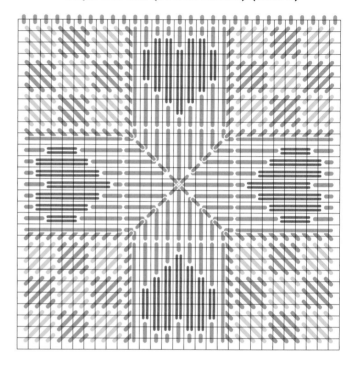

Diaper Box Front/Back (40 x 30 threads) (stitch 2)

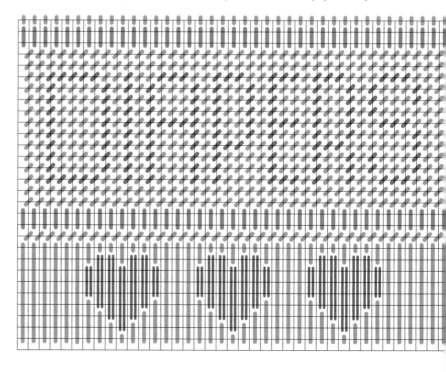

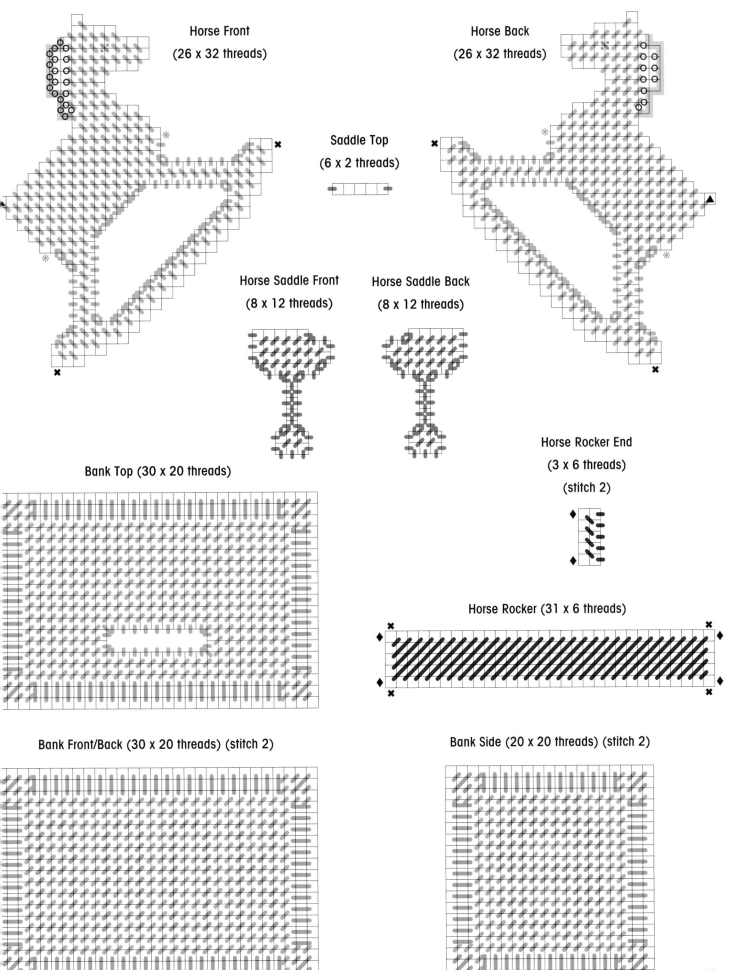

Horse Front
(26 x 32 threads)

Horse Back
(26 x 32 threads)

Saddle Top
(6 x 2 threads)

Horse Saddle Front
(8 x 12 threads)

Horse Saddle Back
(8 x 12 threads)

Horse Rocker End
(3 x 6 threads)
(stitch 2)

Bank Top (30 x 20 threads)

Horse Rocker (31 x 6 threads)

Bank Front/Back (30 x 20 threads) (stitch 2)

Bank Side (20 x 20 threads) (stitch 2)

BABY TISSUE BOX COVER

(Shown on page 29)

Size: 5³/₄"w x 4³/₄"h x 4³/₄"d
(Fits a 5¹/₄"w x 4¹/₄"h x 4¹/₄"d boutique tissue box.)

Supplies: Worsted weight yarn, two 10¹/₂" x 13¹/₂" sheets of clear 7 mesh plastic canvas, and #16 tapestry needle

Stitches Used: Backstitch, Gobelin Stitch, Overcast Stitch, Scotch Stitch, and Tent Stitch

Instructions: Follow charts to cut and stitch pieces. Using white yarn, join one long edge of Front to Top. Join Back to Top. Join Sides to Front, Back, and Top. Cover unworked edges of Tissue Box Cover.

Design by Kooler Design Studio, Inc.

COLOR
white
yellow
pink
blue
green

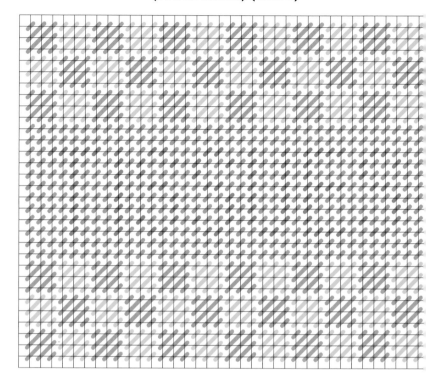

Tissue Box Cover Front/Back/Top
(38 x 32 threads) (stitch 3)

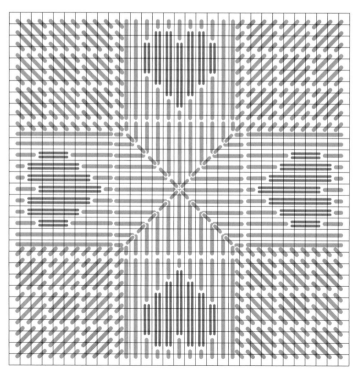

Tissue Box Cover Side #1
(32 x 32 threads)

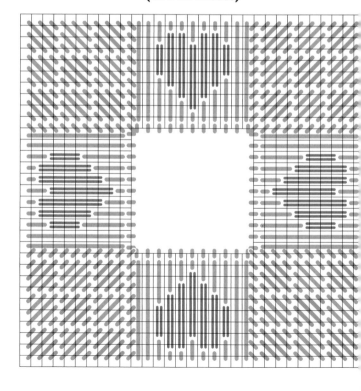

Tissue Box Cover Side #2
(32 x 32 threads)

ot to teen

MONKEY DOOR SIGN

(Shown on page 30)

Size: 6"w x 17³/₄"h

Supplies: Worsted weight yarn, one 10¹/₂" x 13¹/₂" sheet of clear 7 mesh plastic canvas, #16 tapestry needle, and craft glue

Stitches Used: Backstitch, Cross Stitch, French Knot, Gobelin Stitch, Overcast Stitch, and Tent Stitch

Instructions: Follow charts to cut and stitch pieces. Glue Tail to back of Monkey. Glue Flower to Monkey.

Design by Dick Martin.

COLOR	
	pink
	purple
	green
	tan
	lt brown
	brown
	black
	orange French Knot

Flower (4 x 4 threads)

Tail (20 x 45 threads)

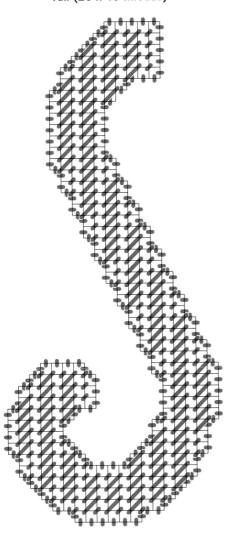

Monkey (41 x 89 threads)

FROG SHELF SITTER

(Shown on page 31)

Size: 3½"w x 9½"h x 2"d

Supplies: Worsted weight yarn, one 10½" x 13½" sheet of clear 7 mesh plastic canvas, #16 tapestry needle, two 12mm moving eyes, 12" of ⅛"w red satin ribbon, and craft glue

Stitches Used: Backstitch, Gobelin Stitch, Overcast Stitch, and Tent Stitch

Instructions: Follow charts to cut and stitch pieces. Use green yarn for all joining.

Cut thirty-six 12" lengths of green yarn.

Place nine lengths together and tie a knot close to one end. With knot on wrong side of Body, thread loose ends through one upper opening in Body. Refer to photo to tie a knot 1½" from Body. Tie a third knot 2¼" from second knot and trim ends. Refer to photo to place knot between Hand Front and Hand Back. Join Hand Front to Hand Back. Repeat for remaining upper opening and Hand pieces.

Place nine lengths of green yarn together and tie a knot close to one end. With knot on wrong side of Body, thread loose ends through one lower opening in Body. Refer to photo to tie a knot 2" from Body. Tie third knot 2½" from second knot and trim ends. Refer to photo to place knot between Foot Front and Foot Back. Join Foot Front to Foot Back. Repeat for remaining lower opening and Foot pieces. Join ends Body together between ▲'s. Join Bottom Body.

Tie ribbon into a bow and trim ends. Glue bow and eyes to Body.

Design by Linda Huffman.

COLOR	
⟋	red
⟋	green

Hand Front

(10 x 8 threads) (stitch 2)

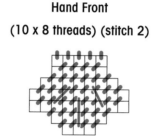

Hand Back

(10 x 8 threads) (stitch 2)

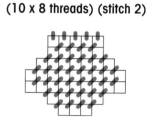

Foot Front

(12 x 10 threads) (stitch 2)

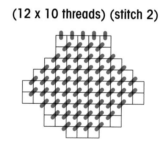

Foot Back

(12 x 10 threads) (stitch 2)

Bottom (17 x 11 threads)

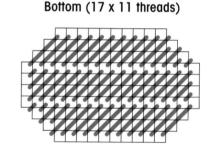

Body (29 x 29 threads)

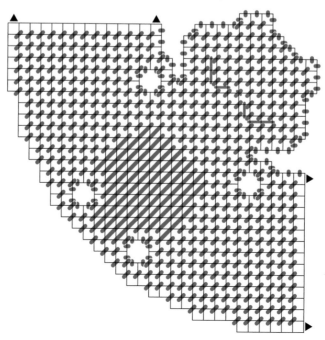

TROPICAL FRAME

(Shown on page 31)

Size: 5³/₄"w x 6"h x 2³/₄"d
(Photo opening is 3"w x 3¹/₄"h.)

Supplies: Sport weight yarn (refer to Master Key), black DMC Embroidery Floss #310, one 10¹/₂" x 13¹/₂" sheet of clear 10 mesh plastic canvas, #20 tapestry needle, and craft glue

Stitches Used: Backstitch, Cross Stitch, French Knot, Gobelin Stitch, Overcast Stitch, and Tent Stitch

Instructions: Follow charts to cut and stitch pieces. Using brown yarn, cover unworked edges of Monkey. Using green yarn, cover unworked edges of Leaves. Using tan yarn, cover unworked edges of Tree Trunk.

For Stand Side #2, cut a Stand Side #1, turn piece over, and cover with lt yellow Tent Stitches. Using lt yellow yarn, join Stand Sides together. Matching ▲'s, tack Stand to Back using lt yellow yarn.

Using yarn color to match Front, join Front to Back along unworked edges. Glue Tree Trunk to Frame. Glue Leaves and Monkey to Frame.

Design by Jenny McCally.

MASTER KEY

	COLOR
⊘	lt yellow
⊘	yellow
⊘	dk yellow
⊘	orange
✎	purple
⊘	blue
⊘	lt green
✎	green
⊘	tan
✎	brown
✎	black floss

Frame Front (55 x 56 threads)

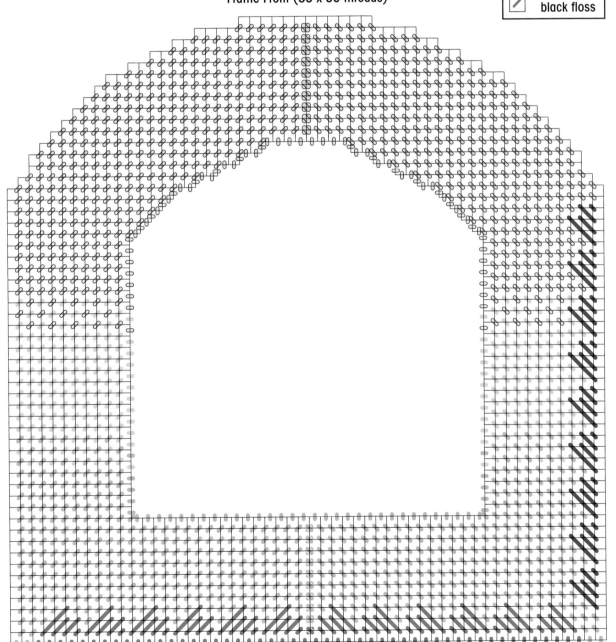

Continued on page 88

	COLOR
⊘	lt yellow
⊘	lt green
⊘	green
⊘	tan
⊘	brown
⊘	brown 2-ply
⊘	black floss - 6 strands
●	black floss French Knot - 6 strands

Back (55 x 56 threads)

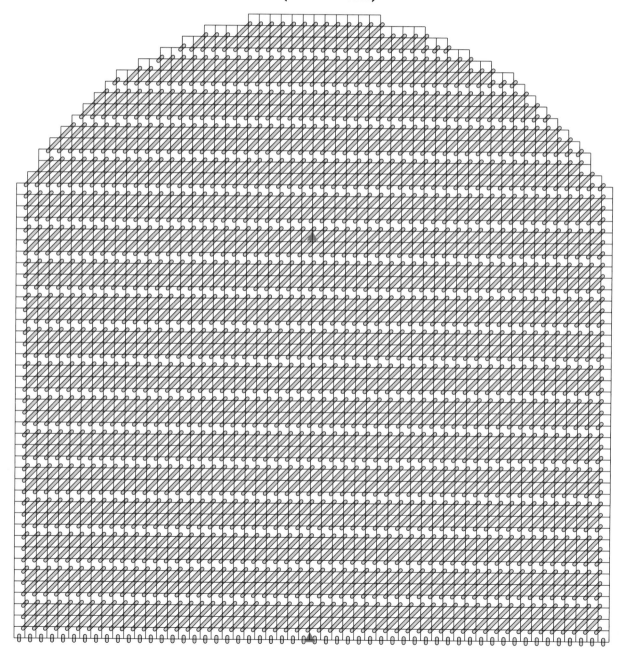

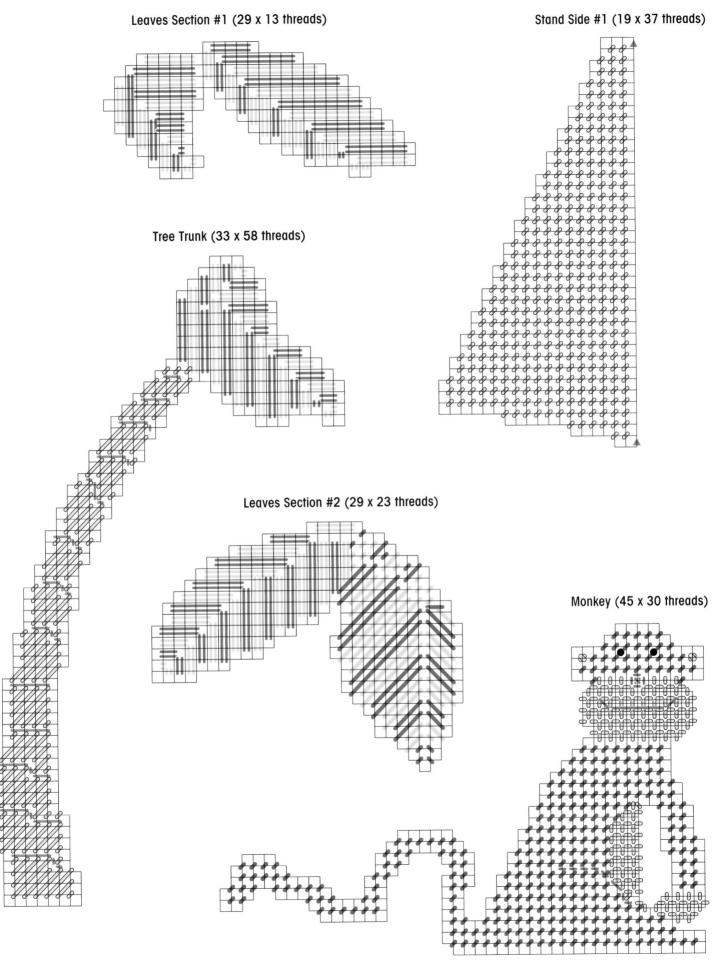

Leaves Section #1 (29 x 13 threads)

Stand Side #1 (19 x 37 threads)

Tree Trunk (33 x 58 threads)

Leaves Section #2 (29 x 23 threads)

Monkey (45 x 30 threads)

GENERAL INSTRUCTIONS

SELECTING PLASTIC CANVAS

Plastic canvas is a molded, nonwoven canvas made from clear or colored plastic. The canvas consists of "threads" and "holes." The threads aren't actually "threads" since the canvas is nonwoven, but it seems to be an accurate description of the straight lines of the canvas. The holes, as you would expect, are the spaces between the threads. The threads are often referred to in the project instructions, especially when cutting out plastic canvas pieces. The instructions for stitches will always refer to holes when explaining where to place your needle to make a stitch.

Types of Canvas. The main difference between types of plastic canvas is the mesh size. Mesh size refers to the number of holes in one inch of canvas. The most common mesh sizes are 5 mesh, 7 mesh, 10 mesh, and 14 mesh. Five mesh means that there are 5 holes in every inch of canvas. Likewise, there are 7 holes in every inch of 7 mesh canvas, 10 holes in every inch of 10 mesh canvas, and 14 holes in every inch of 14 mesh canvas. Seven mesh canvas is the most popular size for the majority of projects.

Your project supply list will tell you what size mesh you need to buy. Be sure to use the mesh size the project instructions recommend.

Most plastic canvas is made from clear plastic, but colored canvas is also available. Colored plastic is ideal when you don't want to stitch the entire background.

When buying canvas, you may find that some canvas is firm and rigid, while other canvas is softer and more pliable. To decide which type of canvas is right for your project, think of how the project will be used. If you are making a box or container, you will want to use firmer canvas so that the box will be sturdy and not buckle after handling. If you are making a tissue box cover, you will not need the firmer canvas because the tissue box will support the canvas and prevent warping. Softer canvas is better for projects that require a piece of canvas to be bent before it is joined to another piece.

Amount of Canvas. The project supply list usually tells you how much canvas you will need to complete the project. When buying your canvas, remember that several different manufacturers produce plastic canvas. Therefore, there are often slight variations in canvas, such as different thicknesses of threads or a small difference in mesh size. Because of these variations, try to buy enough canvas for your entire project at the same time and place. As a general rule, it is always better to buy too much canvas and have leftovers than to run out of canvas before you finish your project. By buying a little extra canvas, you not only allow for mistakes, but have extra canvas for practicing your stitches. Scraps of canvas are also excellent for making magnets and other small projects.

SELECTING YARN

You're probably thinking, "How do I select my yarn from the thousands of choices available?" Well, we have a few hints to help you choose the perfect yarns for your project and your budget.

Yarn Weight. We used various brands of worsted weight yarn to stitch some of the photography models for this book. You may wish to use Needloft® Plastic Canvas Yarn in place of the worsted weight yarn. To help you select colors for your projects, we have included numbers for Needloft yarn in some of our color keys. Needloft yarn is suitable only for 7 mesh plastic canvas. Refer to Types of Yarn for additional information.

Yarn Cost. Cost may also be a factor in your yarn selection. Again, acrylic yarn is a favorite because it is reasonably priced and comes in a wide variety of colors. However, if your project is something extra special, you may want to spend a little more on tapestry yarn or Persian wool yarn to get certain shades of color.

Dye Lot Variations. It is important to buy all of the yarn you need to complete your project from the same dye lot. Although variations in color may be slight when yarns from two different dye lots are held together, the variation is usually apparent on a stitched piece.

Embroidery Floss. Embroidery floss consists of six strands that are twisted together. To ensure smoother stitches, separate the strands of floss and realign them before threading your needle. Refer to the color key or project instructions for the number of strands to use for each project. To help you select colors for your projects, we have included numbers for DMC Embroidery Floss in some of our color keys. If desired, another brand of floss can be substituted for DMC floss.

Yarn Colors. Choosing colors can be fun, but sometimes a little difficult. Your project will tell you what yarn colors you will need. When you begin searching for the recommended colors, you may be slightly overwhelmed by the different shades of each color. Here are a few guidelines consider when choosing your colors.

Consider where you are going to place th finished project. If the project is going in particular room in your house, match yo yarn to the room's colors.

Try not to mix very bright colors with du colors. For example, if you're stitching project using country colors, don't use bright Christmas red with country blues an greens. Instead, use a maroon or count red. Likewise, if you are stitching a brigl tissue box cover for a child's room, dor use country blue with bright red, yellov and green.

Some projects require several shades of color, such as shades of pink for a flowe Be sure your shades blend well together.

Sometimes, you may have trouble findin three or four shades of a color. If you thin your project warrants the extra expense you can usually find several shades of color available in tapestry yarn or Persia wool yarn.

Remember, you don't have to use th colors suggested in the color key. If yo find a red tissue box cover that you reall like, but your house is decorated in blue change the colors in the tissue box cover t blue!

Yarn Yardage Estimator. A handy way c estimating yardage is to make a yar yardage estimator. Cut a one-yard piece c yarn for each different stitch used in you project. For each stitch, work as man stitches as you can with the one-yar length of yarn.

To use your yarn yardage estimator, coun the number of stitches you were able t make, suppose 72 Tent Stitches. Now loo at the chart for the project you want t make. Estimate the number of ecru Ten Stitches on the chart, suppose 150. Nov divide the estimated number of ecru stitche by the actual number stitched with a yard o yarn. One hundred fifty divided by 72 is approximately two. So you will need abou two yards of ecru yarn to make you project. Repeat this for all stitches and yarr colors. To allow for repairs and practice stitches, purchase extra yardage of eacl color. If you have yarn left over, remembe that scraps of yarn are perfect for smal projects such as magnets or when yo need just a few inches of a particular colo for another project.

TYPES OF YARN

Yarn Usage. The first question to ask wher choosing yarn is, "How will my project be sed?" If your finished project will be handled or used a lot, such as a coaster or magnet, you will want to use a durable, washable yarn. We highly recommend acrylic or nylon yarn for plastic canvas. It can be washed repeatedly and holds up well to frequent usage and handling. If your finished project won't be handled or used frequently, such as a framed picture or a bookend, you are not limited to washable yarns.

The types of yarns available are endless, and each grouping of yarn has its own characteristics and uses. The following is a brief description of some common yarns used for plastic canvas.

Worsted Weight Yarn. This yarn may be found in acrylic, wool, wool blends, and a variety of other fiber contents. Worsted weight yarn is the most popular yarn used for 7 mesh plastic canvas because one strand covers the canvas very well. This yarn is inexpensive and comes in a wide range of colors.

Most brands of worsted weight yarn have four plies that are twisted together to form one strand. When the color key indicates "2-ply," separate the strand of yarn and stitch using only two of the four plies.

Needloft® Yarn will not easily separate. When the instructions call for "2-ply" yarn, we recommend that you substitute with six strands of embroidery floss.

Sport Weight Yarn. This yarn has four thin plies that are twisted together to form one strand. Like worsted weight yarn, sport weight yarn comes in a variety of fiber contents. The color selection in sport weight yarn is more limited than in other types of yarns. You may want to use a double strand of sport weight yarn for better coverage of your 7 mesh canvas. Sport weight yarn works nicely for 10 mesh canvas.

Tapestry Yarn. This is a thin wool yarn. Because tapestry yarn is available in a wider variety of colors than other yarns, it may be used when several shades of the same color are desired. For example, if you need five shades of pink to stitch a flower, you may choose tapestry yarn for a better blending of colors. Tapestry yarn is ideal for working on 10 mesh canvas. However, it is a more expensive yarn and requires two strands to cover 7 mesh canvas. Projects made with tapestry yarn cannot be washed.

Persian Wool. This is a wool yarn that is made up of three loosely twisted plies. The plies should be separated and realigned before you thread your needle. Like tapestry yarn, Persian yarn has more shades of

each color from which to choose. It also has a nap similar to the nap of velvet. To determine the direction of the nap, run the yarn through your fingers. When you rub "with the nap," the yarn feels smooth; but when you rub "against the nap," the yarn feels rough. For smoother and prettier stitches on your project, stitching should be done "with the nap." The yarn fibers will stand out when stitching is done "against the nap." Because of the wool content, you cannot wash projects made with Persian yarn.

SELECTING NEEDLES
Stitching on plastic canvas should be done with a blunt needle called a tapestry needle. Tapestry needles are sized by numbers; the higher the number, the smaller the needle. The correct size needle to use depends on the canvas mesh size and the yarn thickness. The needle should be small enough to allow the threaded needle to pass through the canvas holes easily, without disturbing canvas threads. The eye of the needle should be large enough to allow yarn to be threaded easily. If the eye is too small, the yarn will wear thin and may break. You will find the recommended needle size listed in the supply section of each project.

WORKING WITH PLASTIC CANVAS
Throughout this book, the lines of the canvas will be referred to as threads. However, they are not actually "threads" since the canvas is nonwoven. To cut plastic canvas pieces accurately, count **threads** (not **holes**) as shown in **Fig. 1**.

Fig. 1

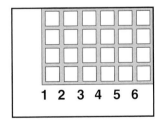

Thread Count. Before cutting your pieces, notice the thread count of each piece on your chart. The thread count is usually located above the piece on the chart. The thread count tells you the number of threads in the width and the height of the canvas piece. Follow the thread count to cut out a rectangle the specified size. Remember to count **threads**, not **holes**. If you accidentally count holes, your piece is going to be the wrong size. Follow the chart to trim the rectangle into the desired shape.

Marking the Canvas. If you find it necessary to mark on the canvas, use an overhead projector pen. Outline shape with pen, cut out shape, and remove markings with a damp paper towel.

Cutting the Canvas. A good pair of household scissors is recommended for cutting plastic canvas. However, a craft knife is helpful when cutting a small area from the center of a larger piece of canvas. For example, a craft knife is recommended for cutting the opening out of a tissue box cover top. When using a craft knife, be sure to protect the table below your canvas. A layer of cardboard or a magazine should provide enough padding to protect your table.

When cutting canvas, be sure to cut as close to the thread as possible without cutting into the thread. If you don't cut close enough, "nubs" or "pickets" will be left on the edge of your canvas. Be sure to cut all nubs from the canvas before you begin to stitch, because nubs will snag the yarn and are difficult to cover.

READING THE COLOR KEY
A color key is included for each project. The key indicates the colors of yarn used and how each color is represented on the chart. For example, when white yarn is represented by a grey line in the color key, all grey stitches on the chart should be stitched using white yarn.

READING THE CHART
Whenever possible, the drawing on the chart looks like the completed stitch. For example, the Tent Stitches on the chart are drawn diagonally across one intersection of threads just like Tent Stitches look on your piece of canvas. Likewise, Gobelin Stitches on the chart look identical to the Gobelin Stitches on your canvas. When a stitch cannot clearly be drawn on the chart, such as a French Knot, a symbol will be used instead. If you have difficulty determining how a particular stitch is worked, refer to Stitch Diagrams, page 92.

JOINING PIECES
Straight Edges. The most common method of assembling stitched pieces is joining two or more pieces of canvas along a straight edge using Overcast Stitches. Place one piece on top of the other with right or wrong sides together. Make sure the edges being joined are even, then stitch the pieces together through all layers.

Continued on page 92

Shaded Areas. The shaded area is part of a chart that has colored shading on top of it. Shaded areas usually mean that all the stitches in that area are used to join pieces of canvas. Do not work the stitches in a shaded area until your project instructions say you should.

Stacking. Sometimes pieces need to be thicker than one layer of canvas. You can do this by stacking. Before you begin stitching, follow your project instructions to stack together plastic canvas pieces so that the edges are even.

Tacking. To tack pieces, run your needle under the backs of some stitches on one stitched piece to secure the yarn. Then run your needle through the canvas or under the stitches on the piece to be tacked in place. The idea is to securely attach your pieces without your tacking stitches showing.

Uneven Edges. Sometimes you'll need to join a diagonal edge to a straight edge. The holes of the two pieces will not line up exactly. Just keep the pieces even and stitch through holes as many times as necessary to completely cover the canvas.

Unworked Threads. Sometimes you'll need to join the edge of one piece to an unworked thread in the center of another piece. Simply place one piece on top of the other, matching the indicated threads or symbols. Join by stitching through both layers.

STITCH DIAGRAMS

> Unless otherwise indicated, bring threaded needle up at 1 and all odd numbers and down at 2 and all even numbers.

ALICIA LACE STITCH
This series of stitches forms a lacy pattern. It consists of simple rows of Tent and Reversed Tent Stitches (**Fig. 2**).

Fig. 2

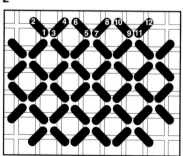

ALTERNATING SCOTCH STITCH
This Scotch Stitch variation is worked over three or more threads, forming alternating blocks (**Fig. 3**).

Fig. 3

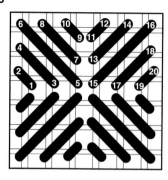

BACKSTITCH
This stitch is worked over completed stitches to outline or define (**Fig. 4**). It is sometimes worked over more than one thread. Backstitch may also be used to cover canvas as shown in **Fig. 5**.

Fig. 4

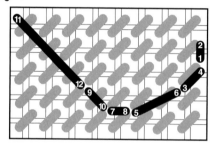

Fig. 5

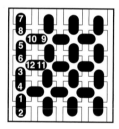

BOXED SCOTCH STITCH
This stitch is composed of a border of Ten Stitches worked around each Scotch Stitc (**Fig. 6**).

Fig. 6

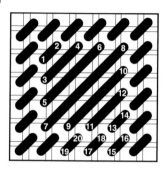

BRAIDED CROSS STITCH
This stitch joins pieces of canvas together Begin by working stitches 1 through (**Fig. 7**). Starting with 4, proceed to wor stitches in **Fig. 8** and **Fig. 9**, working forward over three threads and back ove two. It may be necessary to work extra stitches at corners for better coverage.

Fig. 7

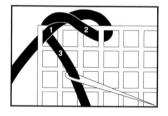

Fig. 8

Fig. 9

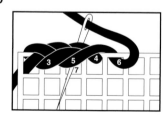

BYZANTINE STITCH

A zigzag effect is created by the Byzantine stitch. It is composed of slanting stitches worked in a diagonal pattern **(Fig. 10)**. The number of threads and intersections covered may vary.

Fig. 10

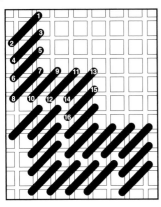

CHECKED SCOTCH STITCH

Scotch Stitch squares alternate with squares of nine Tent Stitches to form this pattern **(Fig. 11)**.

Fig. 11

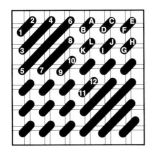

CONDENSED CASHMERE STITCH

This small rectangle pattern is composed of four slanted stitches worked diagonally **(Fig. 12)**.

Fig. 12

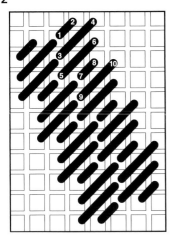

CROSS STITCH

This stitch is composed of two diagonal stitches **(Fig. 13)**. The top stitch of each cross must always be made in the same direction. The number of intersections may vary according to the chart.

Fig. 13

DIAGONAL COUCHING STITCH

This stitch is composed of long diagonal stitches tied down by Reverse Tent Stitches **(Fig. 14)**.

Fig. 14

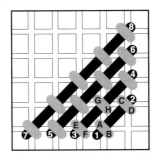

DIAGONAL LEAF STITCH

This stitch is composed of eight straight Gobelin Stitches worked in a counterclockwise direction before adding the long, slanted Gobelin Stitch **(Fig. 15)**. The length of the stitches may vary.

Fig. 15

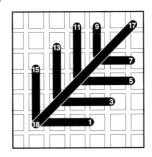

FLAT STITCH

This series of slanted stitches is worked in diagonal rows and has a slightly wavy appearance **(Fig. 16)**.

Fig. 16

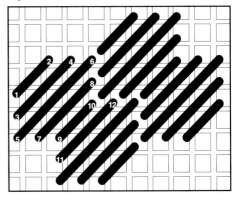

FRENCH KNOT

Bring needle up through hole. Wrap yarn once around needle and insert needle in same hole or adjacent hole, holding end of yarn with non-stitching fingers **(Fig. 17)**. Tighten knot; then pull needle through canvas, holding yarn until it must be released.

Fig. 17

FRINGE STITCH

Fold a length of yarn in half. Thread needle with loose ends of yarn. Bring needle up at 1, leaving a 1" loop on the back of the canvas. Bring needle around the edge of canvas and through loop **(Fig. 18)**. Pull to tighten loop **(Fig. 19)**. Trim strands to desired length from knot. A dot of glue on back of Fringe will help keep stitches in place.

Fig. 18

Fig. 19

Continued on page 94

GOBELIN STITCH

This basic straight stitch is worked over two or more threads or intersections. The number of threads or intersections may vary according to the chart (**Fig. 20**).

Fig. 20

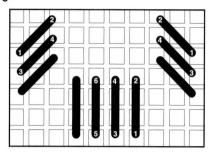

JACQUARD STITCH

Slanted stitches worked over two intersections alternate with Tent Stitches to create this stitch (**Fig. 21**).

Fig. 21

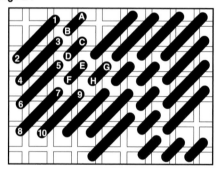

LOOSE OVERCAST STITCH

Worked on top of completed Overcast Stitches, this stitch is worked like the Overcast Stitch to form loops approximately ½" high (**Fig. 22**). It may be necessary to go through the same hole more than once to get an even coverage, especially at the corners.

Fig. 22

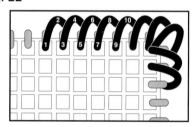

MILANESE STITCH

This stitch is a series of triangular-shaped stitches. The diagonal rows are worked side by side to fill in background areas (**Fig. 23**). The direction of the triangles alternates with each row .

Fig. 23

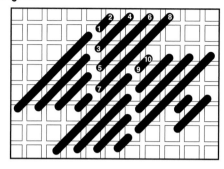

MODIFIED EYELET STITCH

This stitch forms a square over two threads of canvas. It consists of five stitches worked in a clockwise or counterclockwise fashion. Each stitch is worked from the outer edge into the same central hole (**Fig. 24**).

Fig. 24

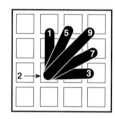

MODIFIED JACQUARD STITCH

Diagonal rows of square-shaped stitches alternate with Tent Stitches to form this pattern (**Fig. 25**).

Fig. 25

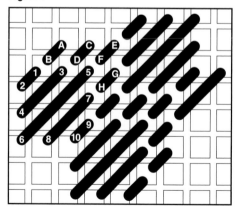

MOSAIC STITCH

This three-stitch pattern forms sma squares (**Fig. 26**).

Fig. 26

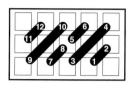

ORIENTAL STITCH

Diagonal rows of triangle-shaped stitches stitched in opposite directions are combine to form this pattern (**Fig. 27**). Fill i between the rows of triangles with rows Gobelin Stitches.

Fig. 27

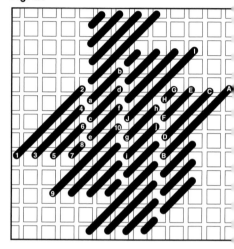

OVERCAST STITCH

This stitch covers the edge of the canva and joins pieces of canvas (**Fig. 28**). may be necessary to go through the same hole more than once to get even coverag on the edge, especially at the corners.

Fig. 28

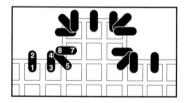

SCOTCH STITCH

This series of slanted stitches, worked over three or more threads, forms squares (Fig. 29).

Fig. 29

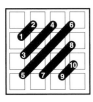

SHELL STITCH

This stitch is composed of three upright stitches drawn together in the middle by a horizontal tie-down stitch (Fig. 30). After working all Shell Stitches, work straight stitches.

Fig. 30

SMYRNA CROSS STITCH

This stitch is worked over two threads as a decorative stitch. Each stitch is worked completely before going on to the next (Fig. 31).

Fig. 31

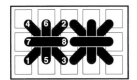

TENT STITCH

This stitch is worked in horizontal or vertical rows over one intersection as shown in **Fig. 32**. Follow **Fig. 33** to work the **Reversed Tent Stitch**. Sometimes when you are working Tent Stitches, the last stitch on the row will look "pulled" on the front of your piece when you are changing directions. To avoid this problem, leave a loop of yarn on the wrong side of the stitched piece after making the last stitch in the row. When making the first stitch in the next row, run your needle through the loop **(Fig. 34)**. Gently pull yarn until all stitches are even.

Fig. 32

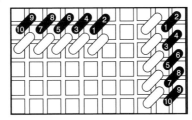

Fig. 33

Fig. 34

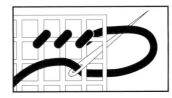

UPRIGHT CROSS STITCH

This stitch is composed one vertical and one horizontal stitch (Fig. 35). Each stitch is worked completely before going on to the next. The direction of the top stitch may vary, but all stitches on a stitched piece should be made in the same direction.

Fig. 35

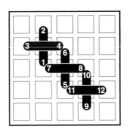

WAFFLE STITCH

This square stitch has a woven look and may be worked over any number of threads (Fig. 36).

Fig. 36

WOUND CROSS STITCH

This stitch has a smooth, circular appearance. Work two horizontal and two vertical stitches into the same central hole (Fig. 37). Bring needle up at 1 and wrap yarn in a circular fashion under all horizontal and vertical stitches. Making sure the yarn lies flat, continue wrapping yarn to fill stitches. Bring needle down at 4 and secure yarn on wrong side of canvas (Fig. 38). The size of the stitch may vary.

Fig. 37

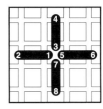

Fig. 38

Instructions tested and photography items made by Toni Bowden, Lylln Craig, Connie Fewell, Carlene Hodge, and Gary Hutcheson.

INDEX